The River Will Be a Part of Us

Justus Wayne Thomas

Daylight

Cofounder: Michael Itkoff
Creative Director: Ursula Damm
Copy Editor: Gabrielle Fastman

© 2024 Daylight Community Arts Foundation

Photographs © 1981 by Justus Wayne Thomas
Photographs © 1981 by Cleg Holiman
Photographs © 1981 by Eva Ohrner-Bauersachs
Photographs © 1981 by Scott Sharp
Photographs © 1981 by Kevin Lowder
Photographs © 1981 by Ed Dilgarde
Text © 2024 by Justus Wayne Thomas
"Black Water Romance" © 2024 by TK Smith

All rights reserved.

ISBN: 978-1-954119-35-2

Printed by Ofset Yapimevi, Turkey

No part of this publication may be reproduced, stored in a retrieval system, or transmitted in any form or by any means without the prior permission in writing of copyright holders and of the publisher.

Daylight Books
E-mail: info@daylightbooks.org
Web: www.daylightbooks.org

For Ed Dilgarde and Cleg Holiman,
our now departed crewmates.

Second star to the right and straight on 'til morning.

J.M. Barrie, *Peter Pan*

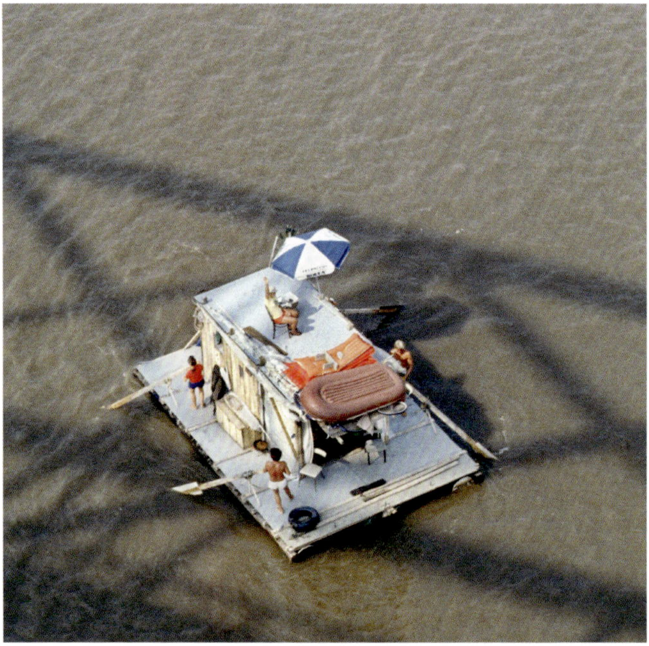

Eulenspiegel
Kansas City to the Atchafalaya River, Louisiana

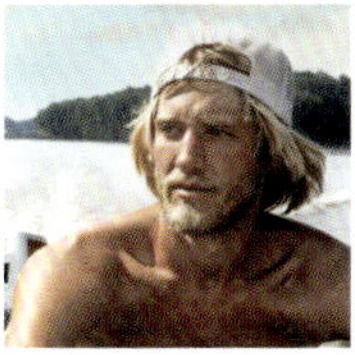

Tom Bates
Kansas City to New Orleans

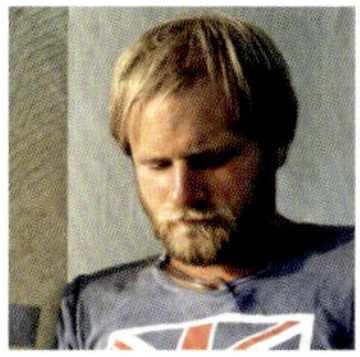

Rick Rottman
Kansas City to St. Louis

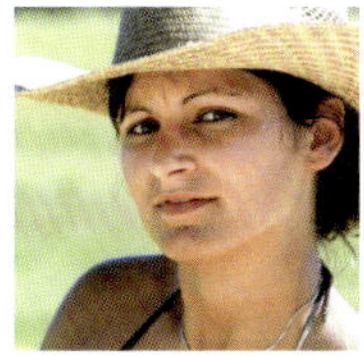

Christa Heinlein
Kansas City to New Orleans

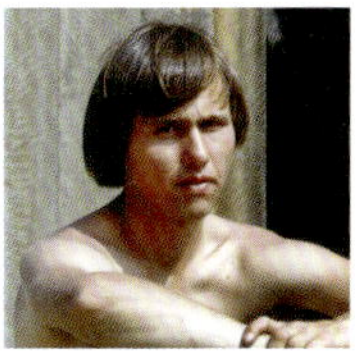

Cleg Holiman
Kansas City to St. Louis

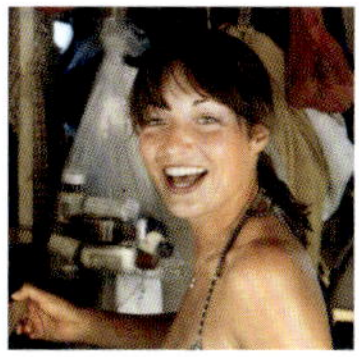

Eva "Evi" Ohrner-Bauersachs
Kansas City to New Orleans

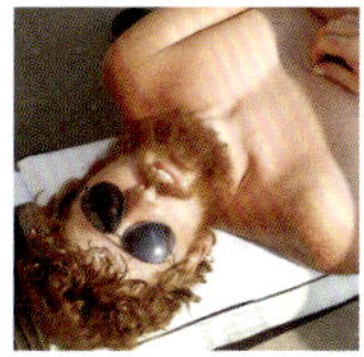

Ed Dilgarde
Kansas City to New Orleans

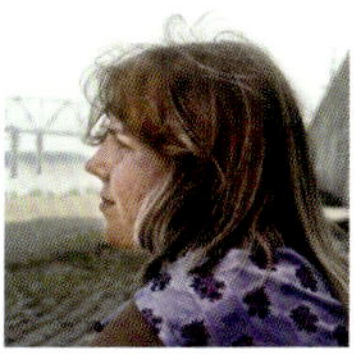

Linda Wenzek-Barth
St. Louis to Memphis

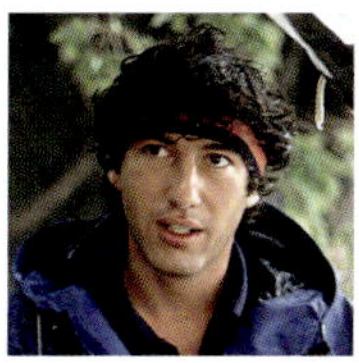

Jeff James
Chester, IL, to New Orleans

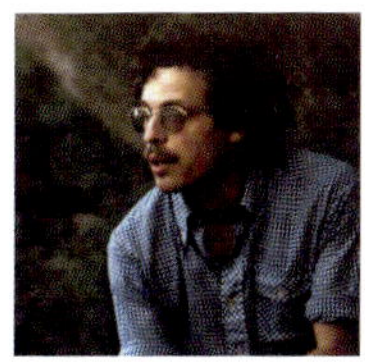

Scott Sharp
Kansas City to Jefferson City, MO

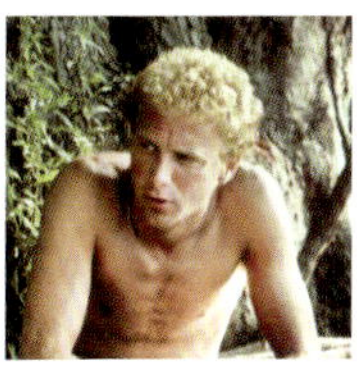

Bill Chase
St. Louis to Memphis

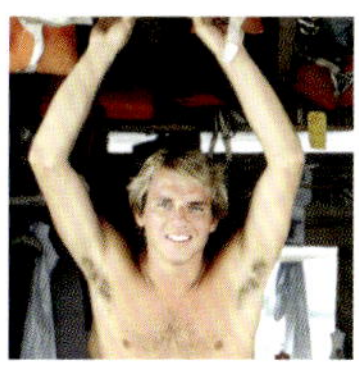

Kevin Lowder
St. Louis to Chester, IL

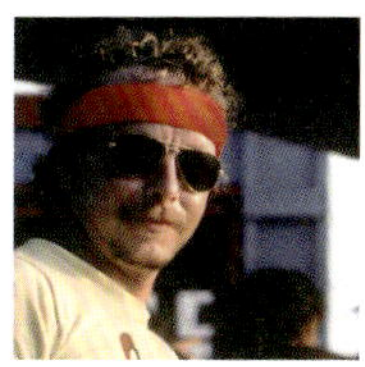

Michael Bailey
Natchez, MS, to New Orleans

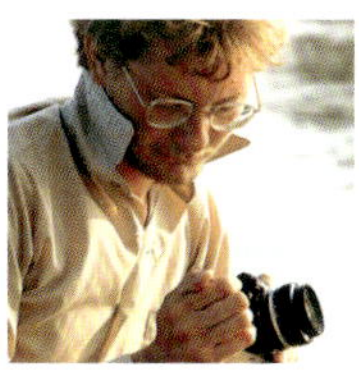

Justus Wayne Thomas
Kansas City to New Orleans

BLACK WATER ROMANCE

It is romantic to imagine a group of friends leisurely floating down the Mississippi River on a raft they built with their own hands. Skin browning from exposure to the sun, they lounge along the raft's wooden deck and let the current pull them along. Of course there would be laughter, perhaps as they shared their meals, and one can also imagine heated debates over the great philosophical questions: What is love? What is free will? Does the soul exist?

A great journey from Kansas City to New Orleans by way of the Missouri River and the mighty Mississippi is the stuff of mythology, fables from the days of fur traders and pioneers told around campfires and in the lyrics of folk songs. However fanciful it may seem, in 1981 photographer Justus Wayne Thomas and an assortment of friends, new and old, built a raft and embarked on their own twentieth-century epic, poetically captured in photographs.

Thomas, who was born and raised in Nashville, had almost no relationship to water, with no desire or ideation for floating before 1981. Shortly after graduating from Vanderbilt University, he was invited by his college friend Tom Bates to document a float trip—a leisurely cruise down a river by innertube, canoe, or raft—with his camera. The precedent for the trip occurred in 1979 during Thomas's junior year studying abroad in an exchange program at the University of Regensburg in West Germany. Bates floated down the Danube River on an inflatable raft with a group of friends and was inspired to plan a float trip for the great rivers of the United States. Although Thomas did not join the initial trip, he did spend his time abroad taking photographs using the Minolta SRT 201 that he borrowed from his parents. Never formally taught, Thomas honed his skills by creating photographs of Regensburg's landscape and architecture, benefiting from a small darkroom found in the basement of student accommodations. When the call came in 1981, he packed his camera and a copy of *The Adventures of Huckleberry Finn* and headed west. The plan was to embark just outside Kansas City, Missouri, and float to New Orleans, Louisiana, on the Missouri and the Mississippi.

The trip resulted in a series of photographs belonging to the documentary photography genre that were captured by Thomas and other members of the crew. The genre is defined by its commitment to accurate representations of life and events. Thomas's mission was to capture the experience of the journey in photographs that would be used to illustrate a book that Bates had intended to write but never did; the journal he kept to document the trip was tragically lost to the river during the final days of the journey. Through these lasting images, we can visualize the various logistics that made the seemingly improbable journey possible, as well as gain a sense of how it felt for the crew along the way. Thomas made images documenting the ten-day construction of the raft in LaBenite Park near Independence, Missouri. The two-ton behemoth consisted of a 16' x 24' deck built with 6" x 6" lumber beams and two rigor beams made from a halved telephone pole. The wooden frame sat atop thirty-two 55-gallon empty and sealed oil drums, banded beneath the frame to keep the raft afloat. The raft had no motor and was steered by four 10-foot oars attached to the four corners of the deck. We see in the photographs that it would take one's full body weight to drag the oar through the water. Atop the main deck sat a 48-square-foot cabin constructed of cottonwood that held food, books, clothing, and supplies. Dispelling any allusions to Huck Finn's makeshift raft made from fine pine planks, Thomas's images show us a sturdy vessel equipped with a transistor radio, an inflatable lifeboat, and a small gas oven.

The raft launched on July 3, 1981. Thomas used his lens to capture sprawling landscapes and aerial views of the raft floating along the river. Appearing small and insignificant amidst the choppy waters, he photographed the raft from the high vantage point of a nearby bridge. He captured the raft tethered along sandy banks, the wood appearing stark against pearly skies and low verdant horizon lines. Sleeping was done on deck; some members of the crew slept in sleeping bags and all-weather coats, and there were also air-cushion bags to rest on. The raft would typically be anchored at night while the crew slept, bobbing just a few feet from the river's shore. It would also be tethered while they ventured out to gather supplies from local towns and cities. Thomas captured not only the crew's treks through grassy fields and back roads but also abandoned storefronts and decaying architecture, preserving views of businesses and buildings along the rivers that may now be lost to time.

The dominant subjects of Thomas's photographs are his fellow crew members. As he recounts, "Most of the pictures taken were of me on the raft with these people. That was 90% of the experience. What I wound up with were more pictures that focused on individuals. In retrospect, all my crewmates were beautiful, very handsome people, very expressive and good to take pictures of. They knew I was there, and they were comfortable with my camera."

He captured an intimacy in his documentation, both in visual tone and literal physical proximity, that creates a similar effect to that of a family's private photo album. Amidst such an expansive natural backdrop, Thomas's images captured a strong sense of domesticity. There are beautiful images of crew members washing themselves in the murky river water, cutting each other's hair, reading together from books they shared, and cooking meals together. Thomas's images capture the long, lean bodies of the crew in action as they manned the raft but also in the low moments, draped over wooden chairs and benches. One can imagine rich conversation but also long stretches of silence, possibly interrupted by the buzz of mosquitoes and the occasional fish jumping in the water. Thomas captured his fellow crew members with eyes often averted from the lens, which emphasizes the sense of stillness and a growing trust. To keep the raft afloat, the crew had to move collectively, depending on each other for survival. These bonds were formed in the unimaginable slow and sticky pace of floating along at the river's whim. It is clear to see across the photographs that if they had not been family before the trip in 1981, they are surely family now.

Placing the photographs in an art-historical context, there is an immediate connection to the practice of landscape painter George Caleb Bingham (1811–1879). Bingham was known for his depictions of what was then the Western frontier of the burgeoning United States. Just like Thomas, Bingham was essentially a self-taught artist, though he studied for three months at the Pennsylvania Academy of the Fine Arts, and in 1856, much like Thomas, traveled to Germany to study the masters of the Düsseldorf school. A source for the romantic nature of Bingham's landscapes, the Düsseldorf school was a group of painters whose work is characterized by sentimentality and careful attention to detail. Some of his most known works depict river scenes in which men float on wooden rafts carrying the commerce of the day. *Raftsmen Playing Cards* (1847) depicts a slow-paced moment along the Missouri as the raft crew entertains themselves with card games, and *The Jolly Flatboatmen* (1846) captures a raucous moment of dancing atop the flat-roofed cabin of a wooden raft. Bingham was known as a part of the luminist movement in landscape painting, a style popularized in the 1850s and defined by aerial perspectives and attention to the nuance of natural light. The subject of luminist paintings emphasizes tranquility, slowness, and stillness, often shown through elements of nature like calm flowing waters, soft endless skies, and low-action scenes. Thomas's photographs could easily fit in the luminist camp, especially given his use of Kodak Ektachrome film, known for capturing natural light well and creating rich saturated color in fine-grain photographs. This film is what gives the photographs their texture and majestic quality.

The feelings of romance conjured by Thomas's photographs come not simply from their visual beauty but from the content's context within the visual culture of the United States. The images create an immediate sense of nostalgia for something yearned for but rarely experienced—adventure. Many Americans, especially those living in the Midwest and South, take float trips down rivers and streams in the summertime for fun. To float the Missouri and the Mississippi, two iconic rivers steeped in the ideologies of westward expansion and histories of global commerce and war, takes a stance beyond leisure. The fidelity of time slips across the images, and few visual clues help to tell us exactly when the trip occurred. The shaggy-haired men and bikini-clad women let us know we are sometime past the 1950s but these photographs could have easily been taken in the early 1990s. Along with the Greenpeace sign that adorns the cabin and the Pabst Blue Ribbon can clutched in a crew member's fist, these images become part of the larger American iconography, speaking to a particular feeling more so than a particular historical event. Thomas used his camera to capture not only a moment in time but the mythological spirit that the country was founded on. The tale of the 1981 float trip is a black water romance, a historical myth where facts and details are lost over time but meaning is gained.

—TK Smith

TK Smith is an Atlanta-based curator, writer, and cultural historian.

EULENSPIEGEL

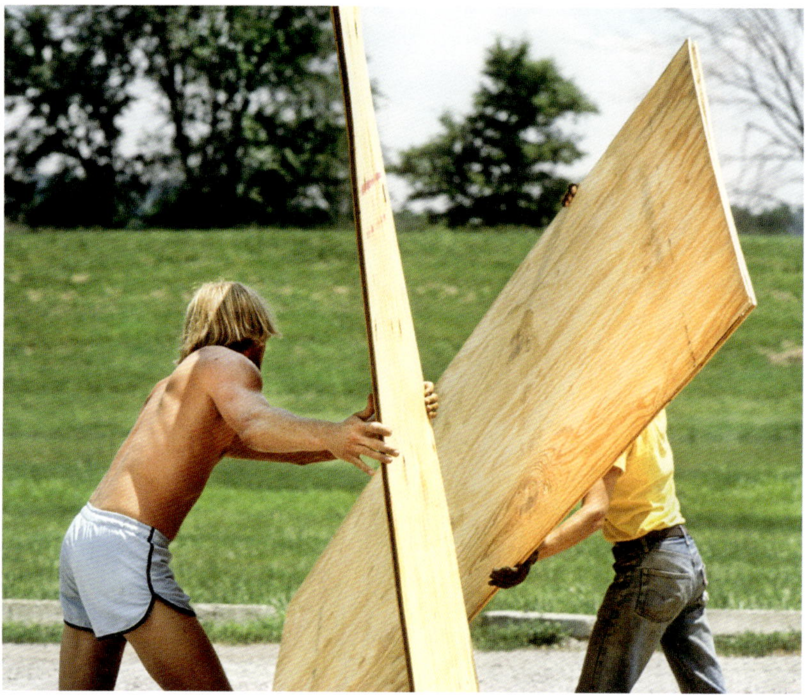

It would be the summer of Princess Diana's wedding. The space shuttle had just completed its first mission, and *Raiders of the Lost Ark* was running in theaters. Handheld mobile phones were years away, and no one had ever heard of the internet. In late June of 1981, a motley assortment of young people from the United States and Germany gathered at a small park on the banks of the Missouri River, just outside Kansas City.

The month before, I had been at home in Nashville when I got a telephone call from Tom Bates. We had become friends a few years before as American exchange students at the University of Regensburg in West Germany. Tom asked if I was interested in joining him and some other friends at a campsite near Kansas City, where they planned to build a raft and float down the Missouri and the Mississippi Rivers to New Orleans.

A commitment like this would require money that I did not have, so I asked my parents. My mom was hesitant, but my dad said:

"He's going. If I have to carry him up to Kansas City on my back, he's going."

I took a plane instead.

When I arrived, Tom Bates, Ed Dilgarde, Rick Rottman, Evi Orhner, Christa Heinlein, and Cleg Holiman were already at LaBenite Park in Sugar Creek, Missouri, just a few miles downriver from Kansas City, preparing to build a 16' x 24' raft from assorted lumber, plywood, a telephone pole, and some 55-gallon oil drums. We designed and built our raft in ten days and launched on July 3, 1981.

For the next two months, we dodged barges, scraped over wing dikes, slammed into a pier, battled fierce storms and fiercer mosquitoes, got stuck on a sandbar, sucked into a chute, and were nearly killed trying to tie up at night next to a showboat in St. Louis. But mostly, we floated, talked, read, explored, and met people we would never see again.

We collaborated, argued, and took care of one another.

After some extended debate between Kansas City and St. Louis, we decided to christen our floating home *Eulenspiegel*, after a traveling trickster and jester from medieval German folklore.

—Justus Wayne Thomas

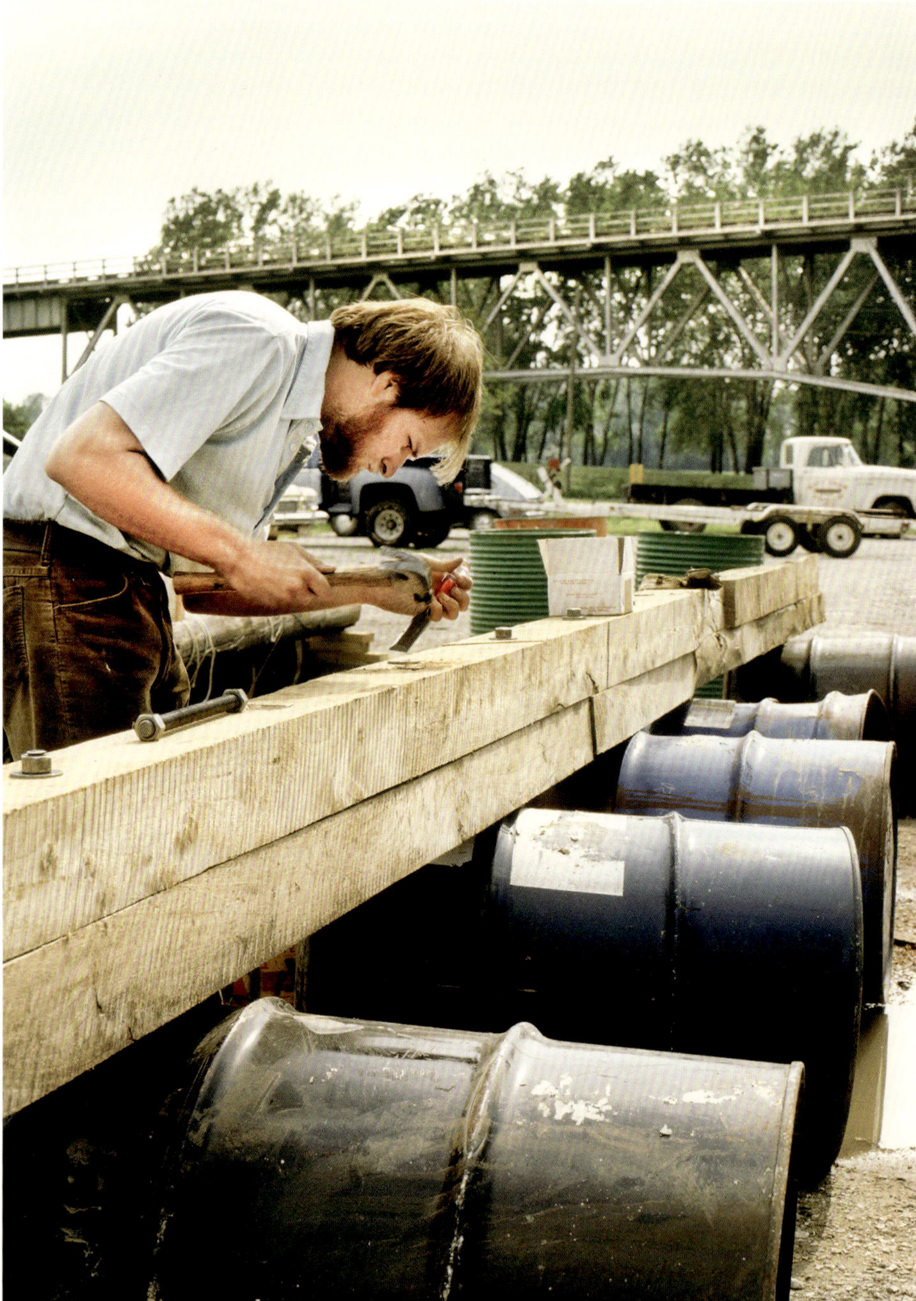

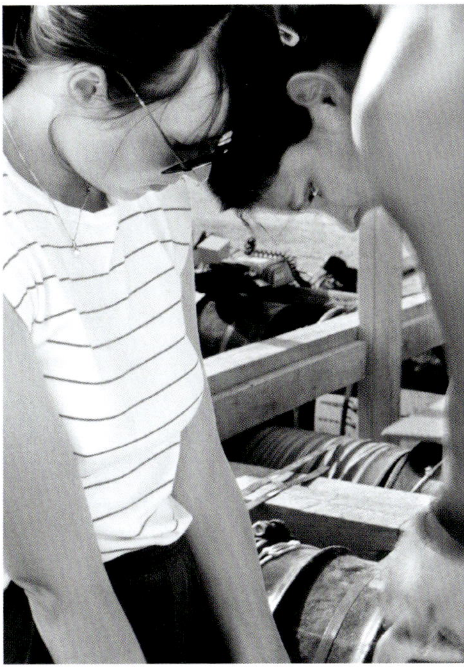
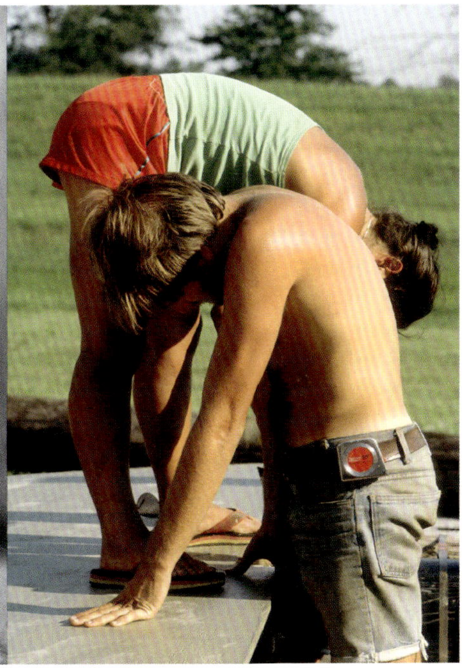

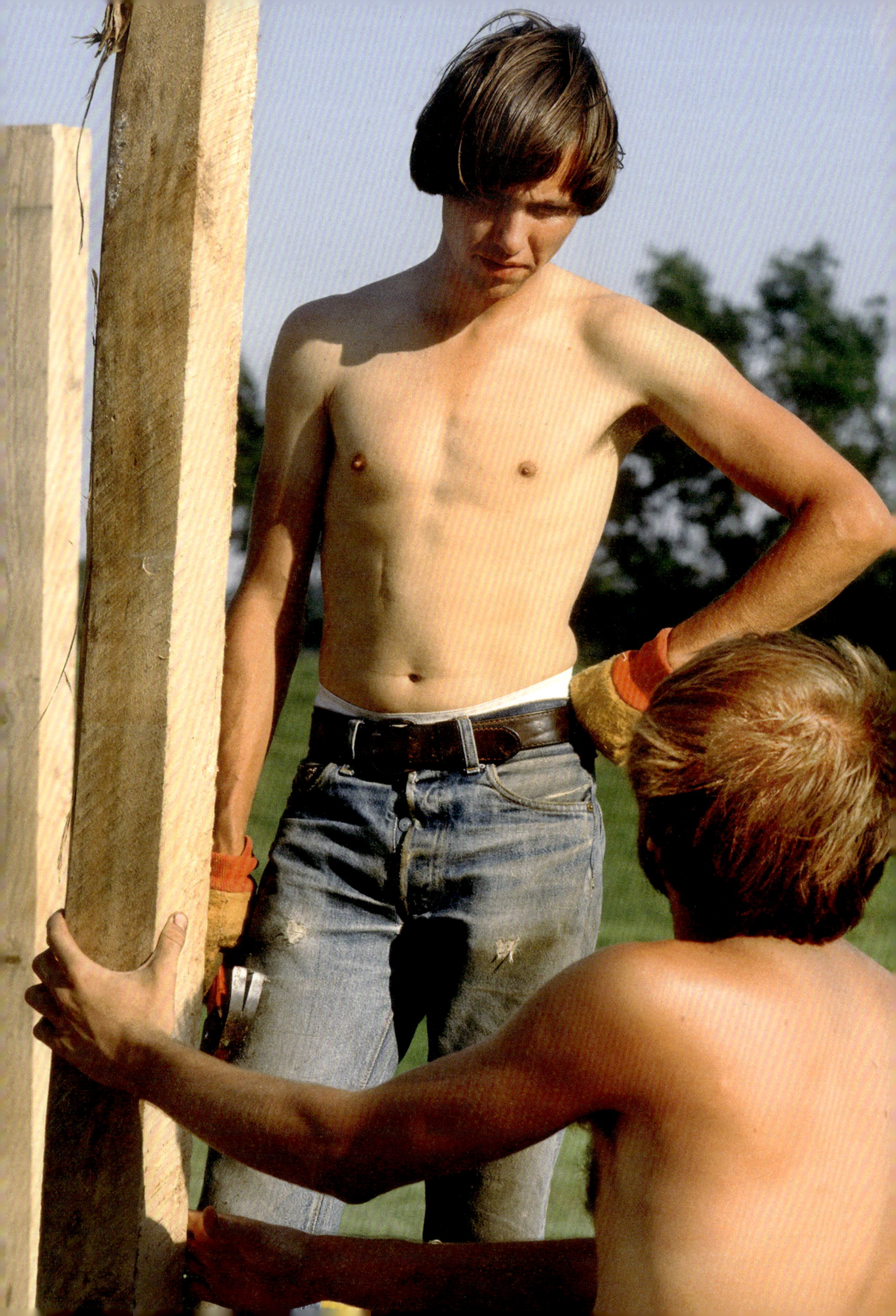

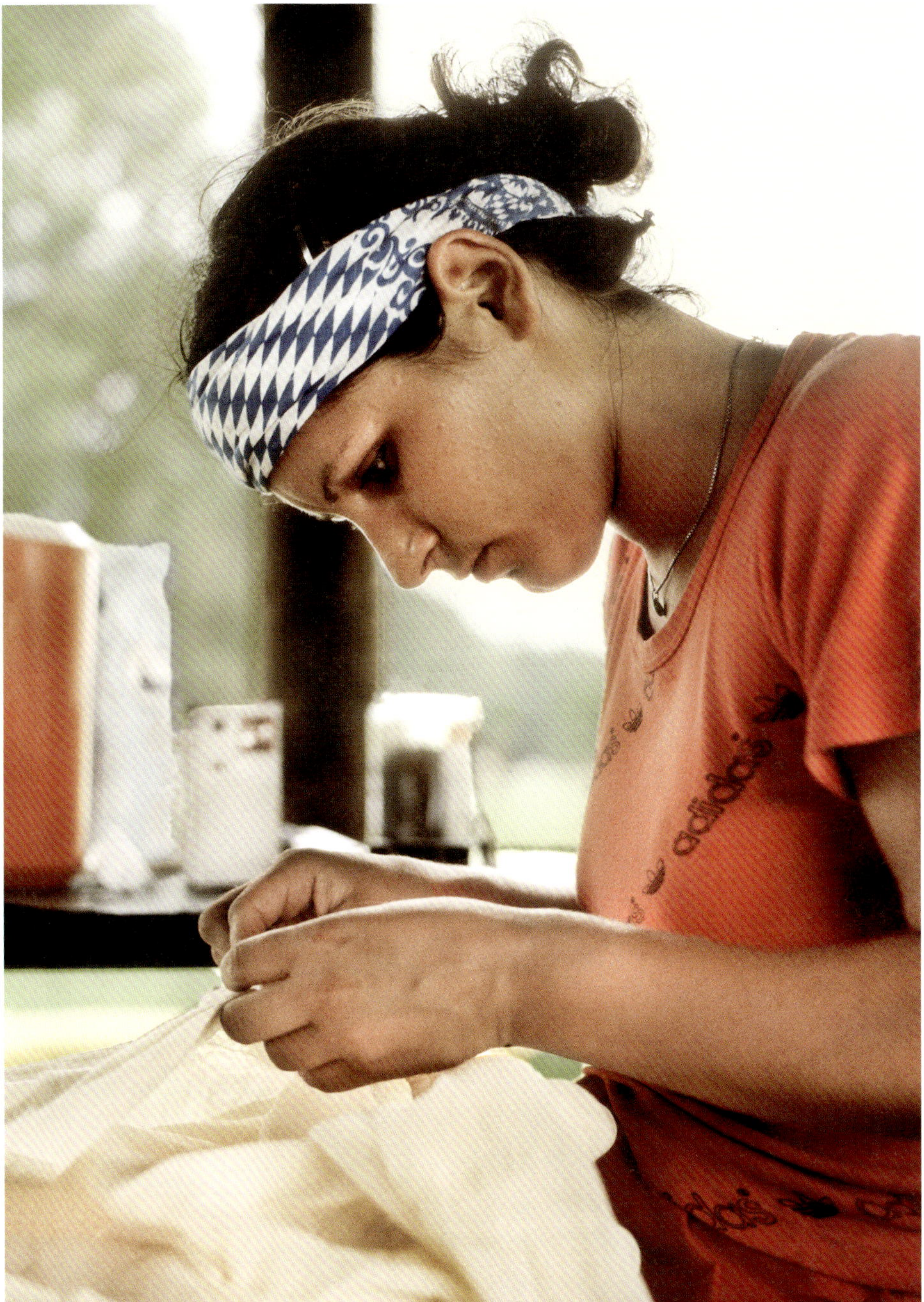
adidas

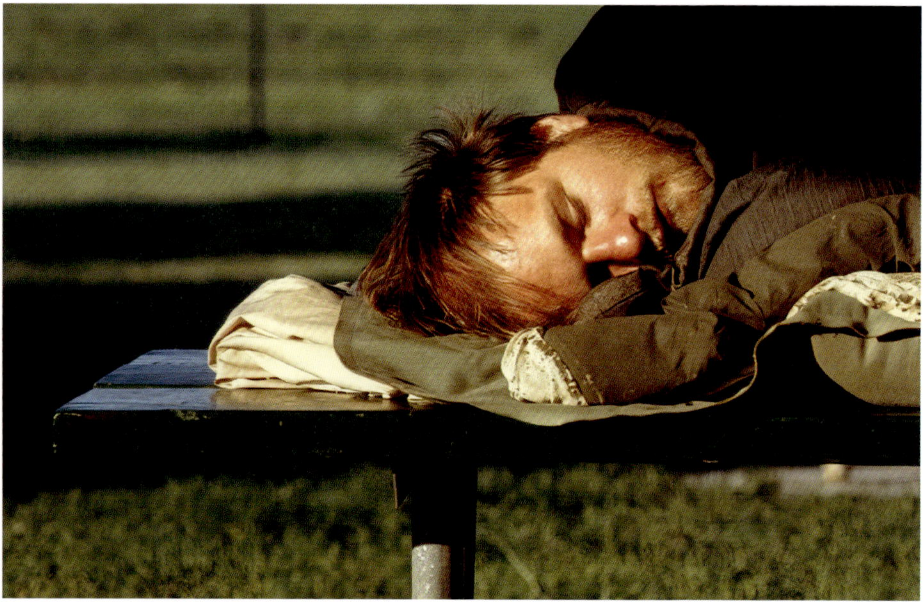

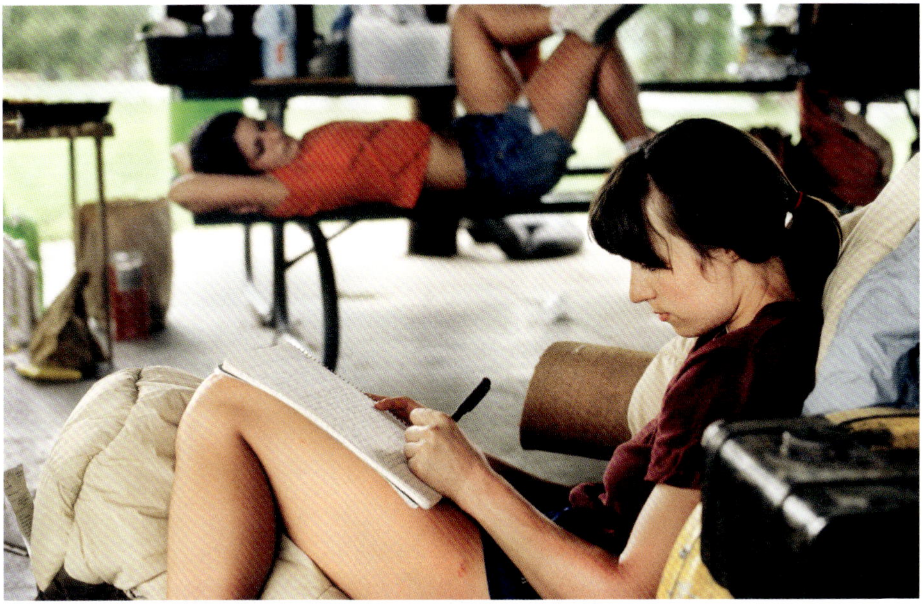

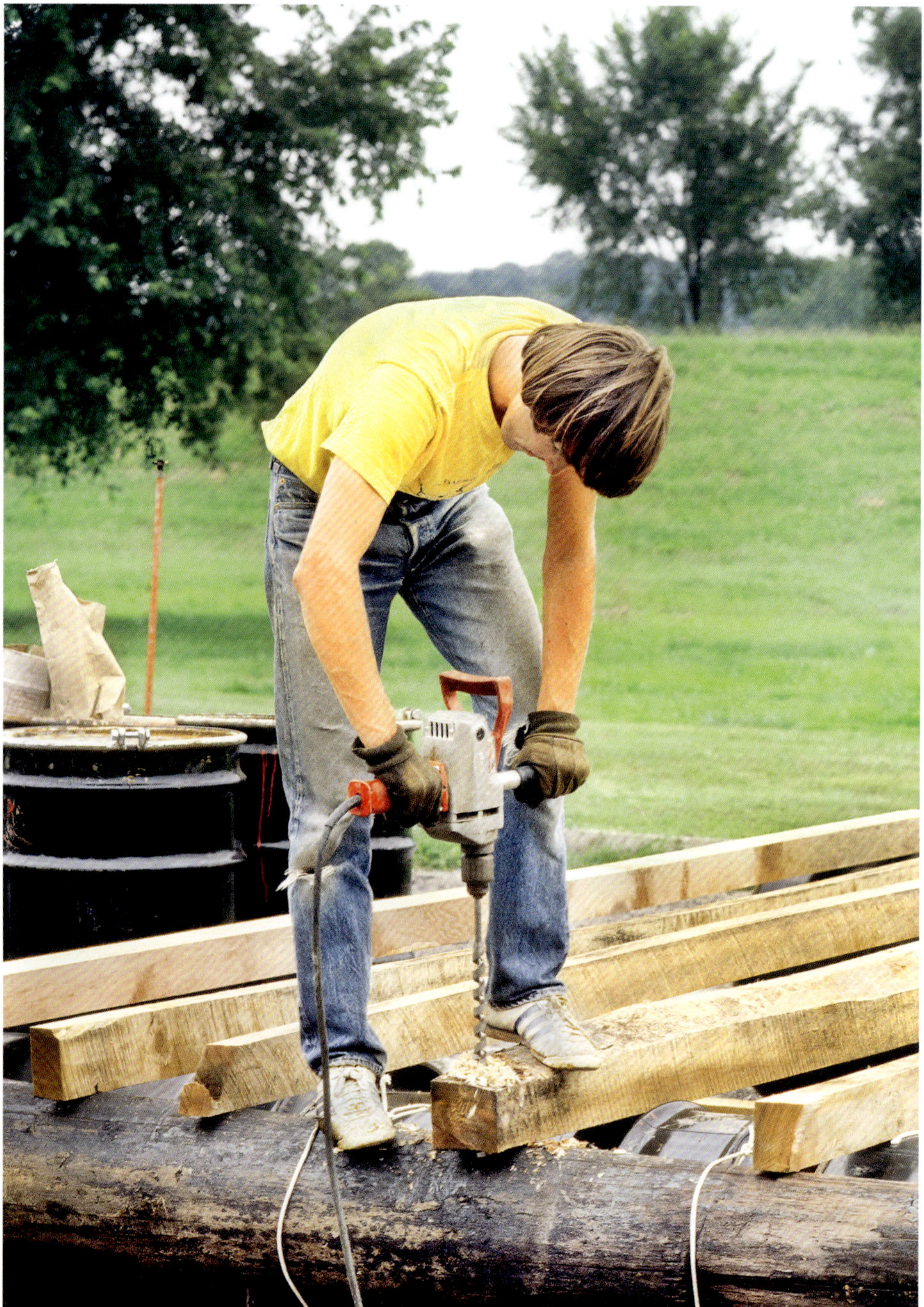

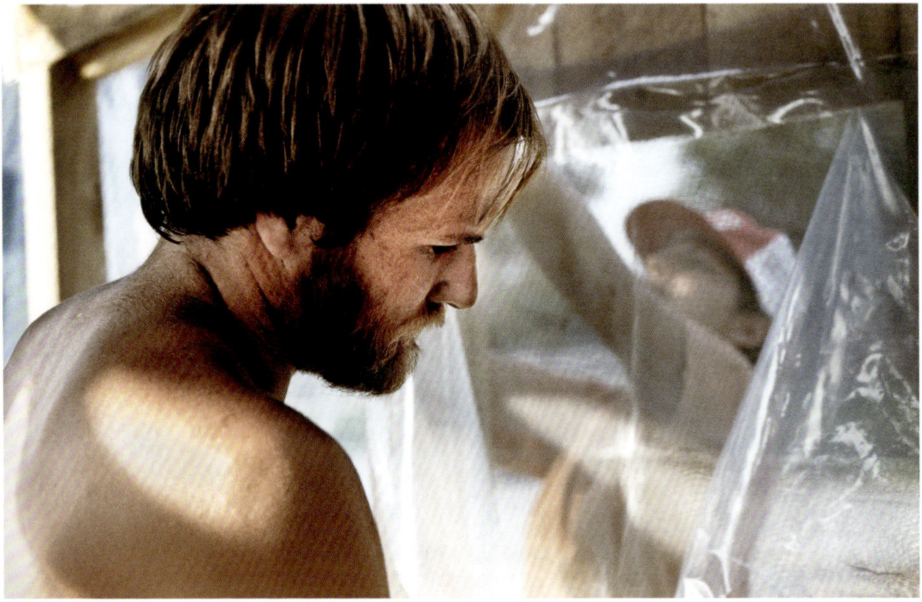

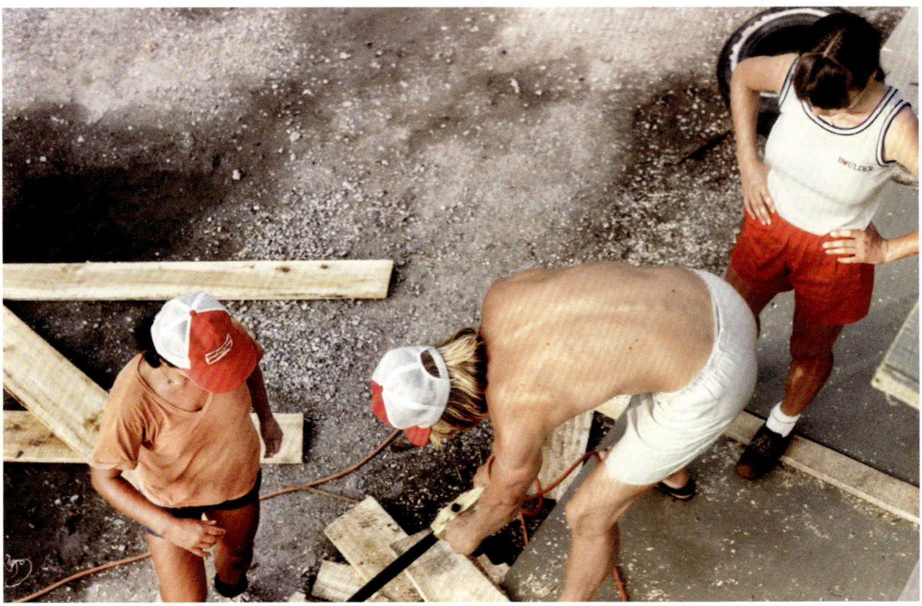
BOULDER

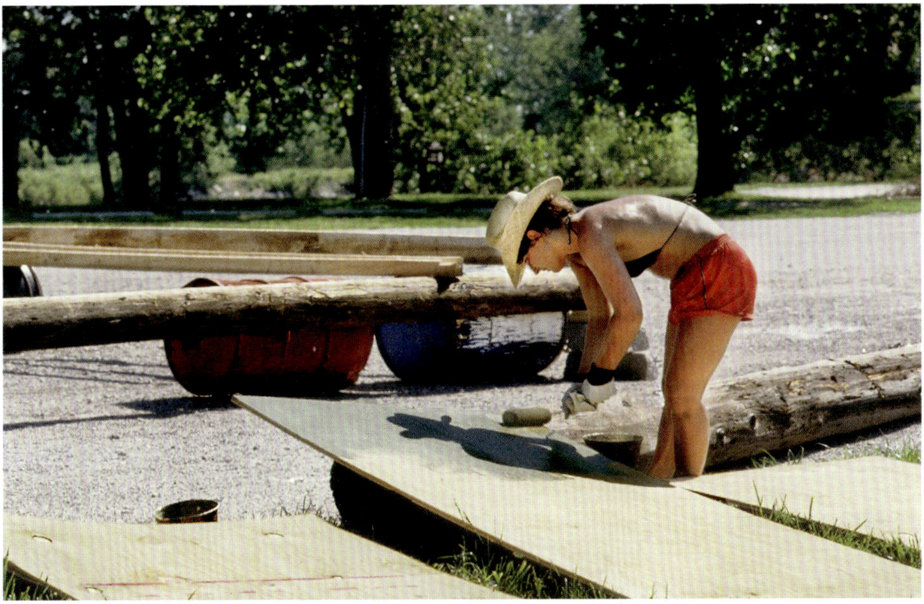

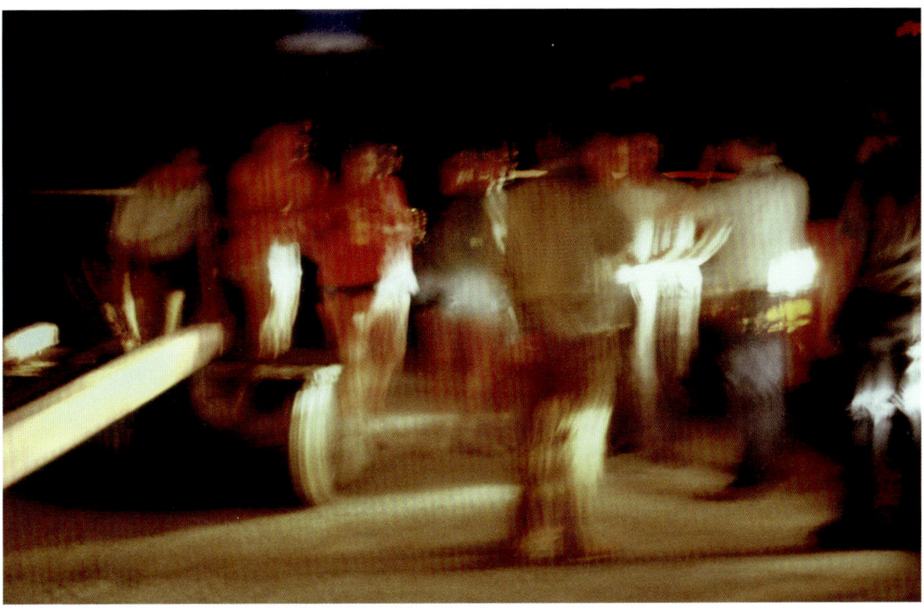

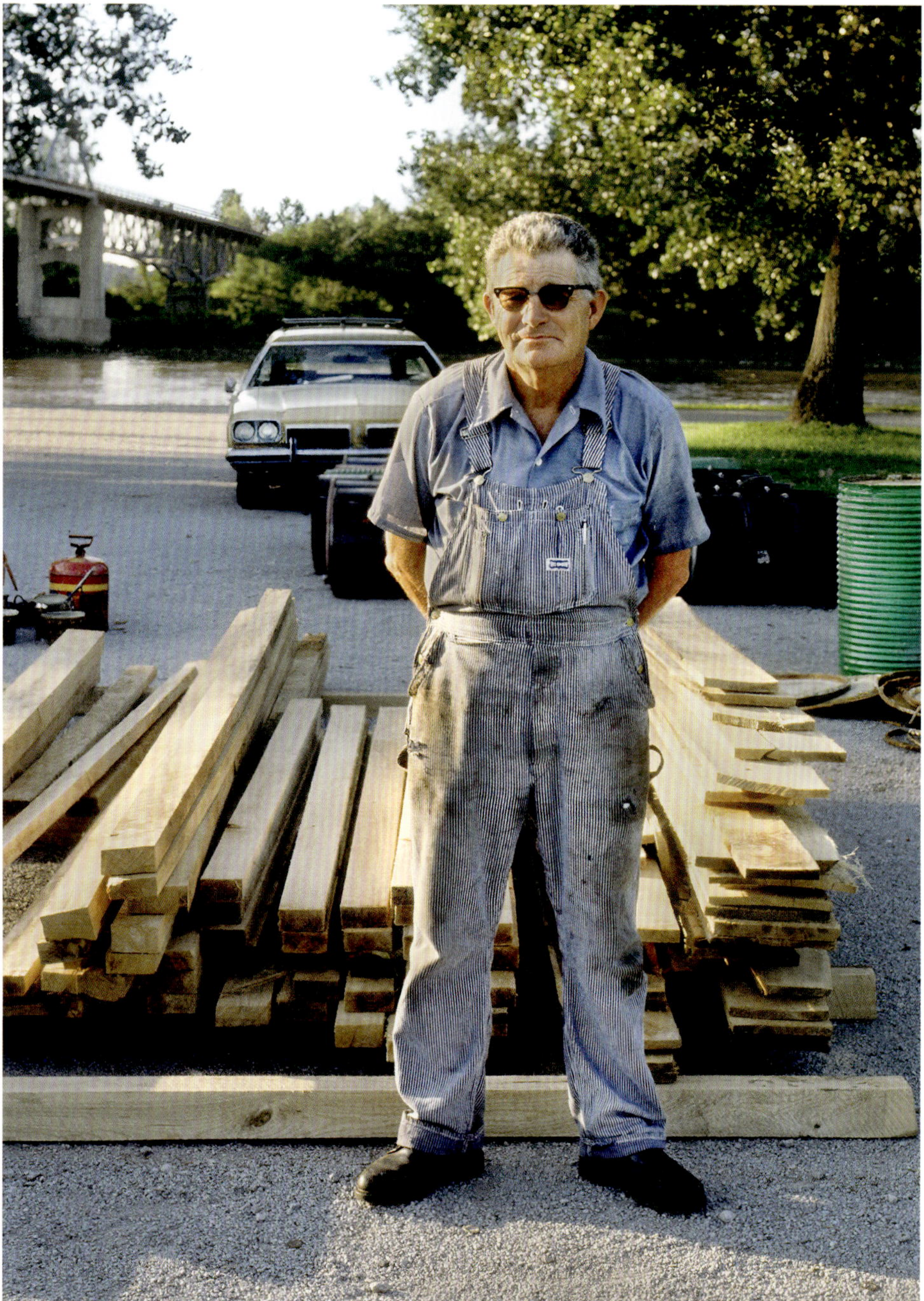

Delbert Fisher supplied us with rough-cut cottonwood lumber from trees he felled himself and cut to order. Delbert's makeshift lumberyard was in his backyard, behind his double-wide trailer, atop the limestone cliffs overlooking the Missouri River. We used this lumber to build the raft's cabin and support timbers on top of the deck frame.

Delbert's total bill, including gas for delivery to the site in his pickup, was ninety dollars.

Eno Mewes, a Kansas City businessman who had emigrated from Germany, came down to LaBenite Park and gave us $500. He said he had seen the TV news spots about the raft trip and wanted to help us do something he had always wanted to do.

Later, an old woman approached Christa and said, "I wish I still could do what you're about to do."

We came to realize that we would be carrying people along with us in spirit.

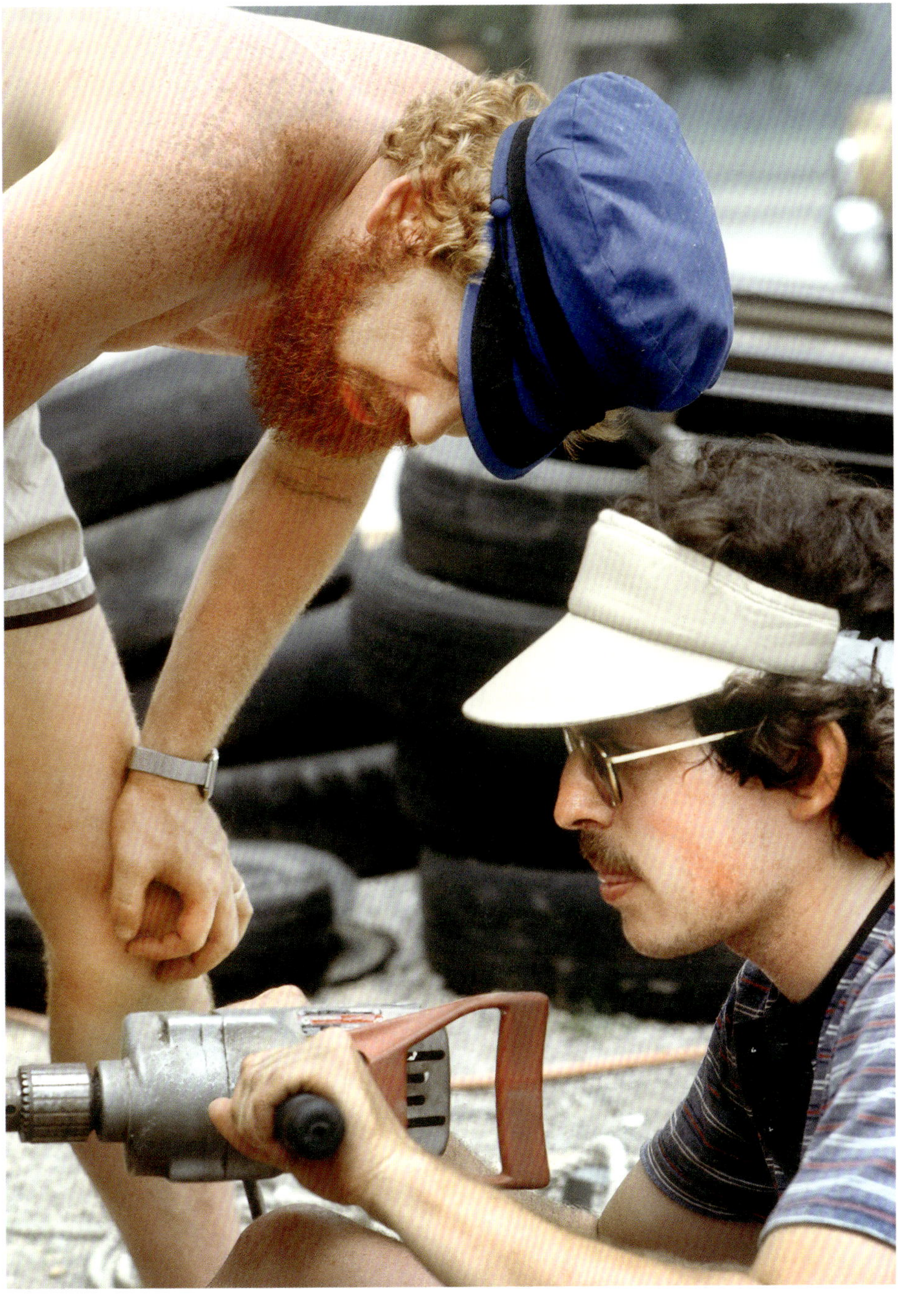

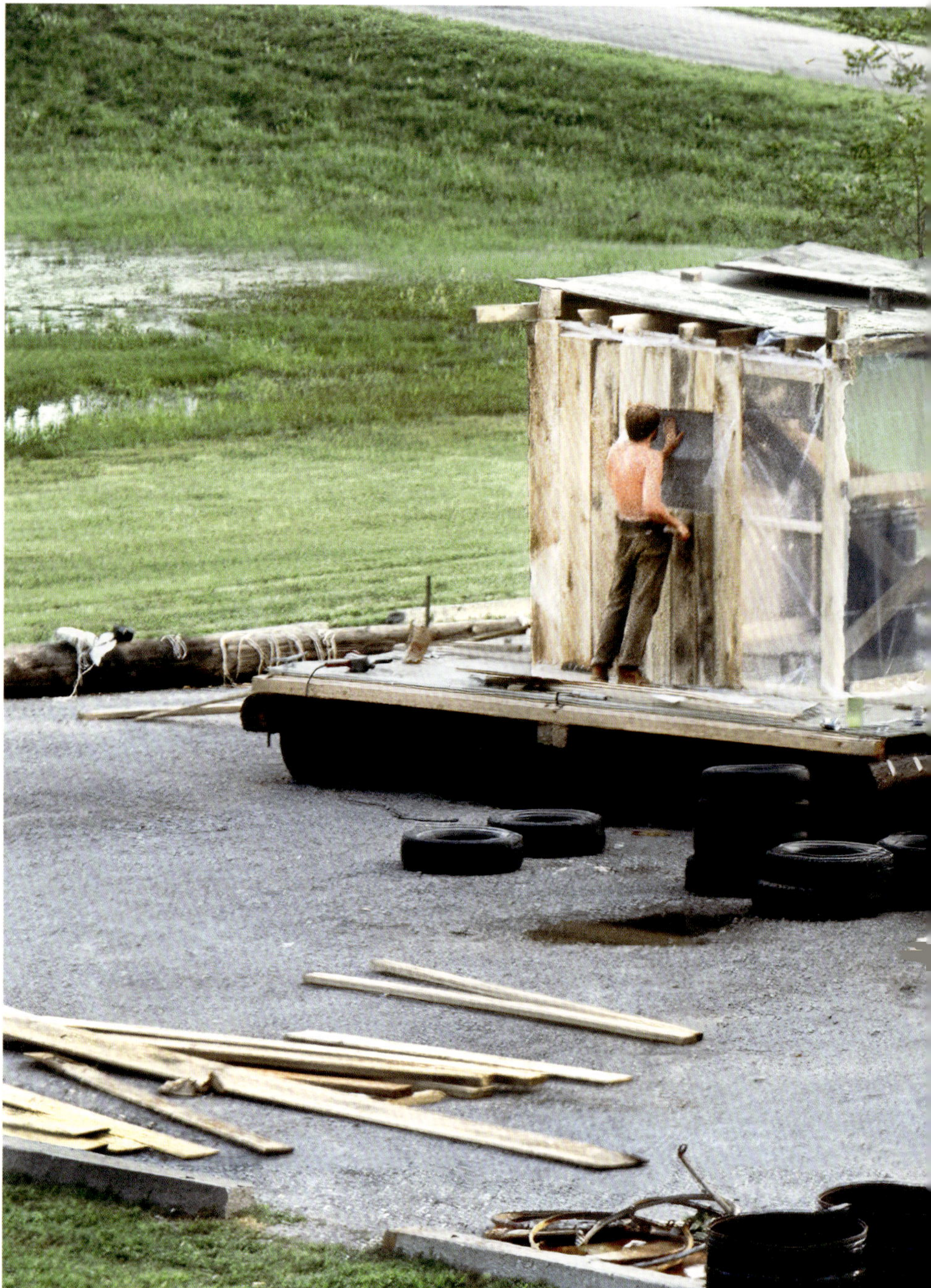

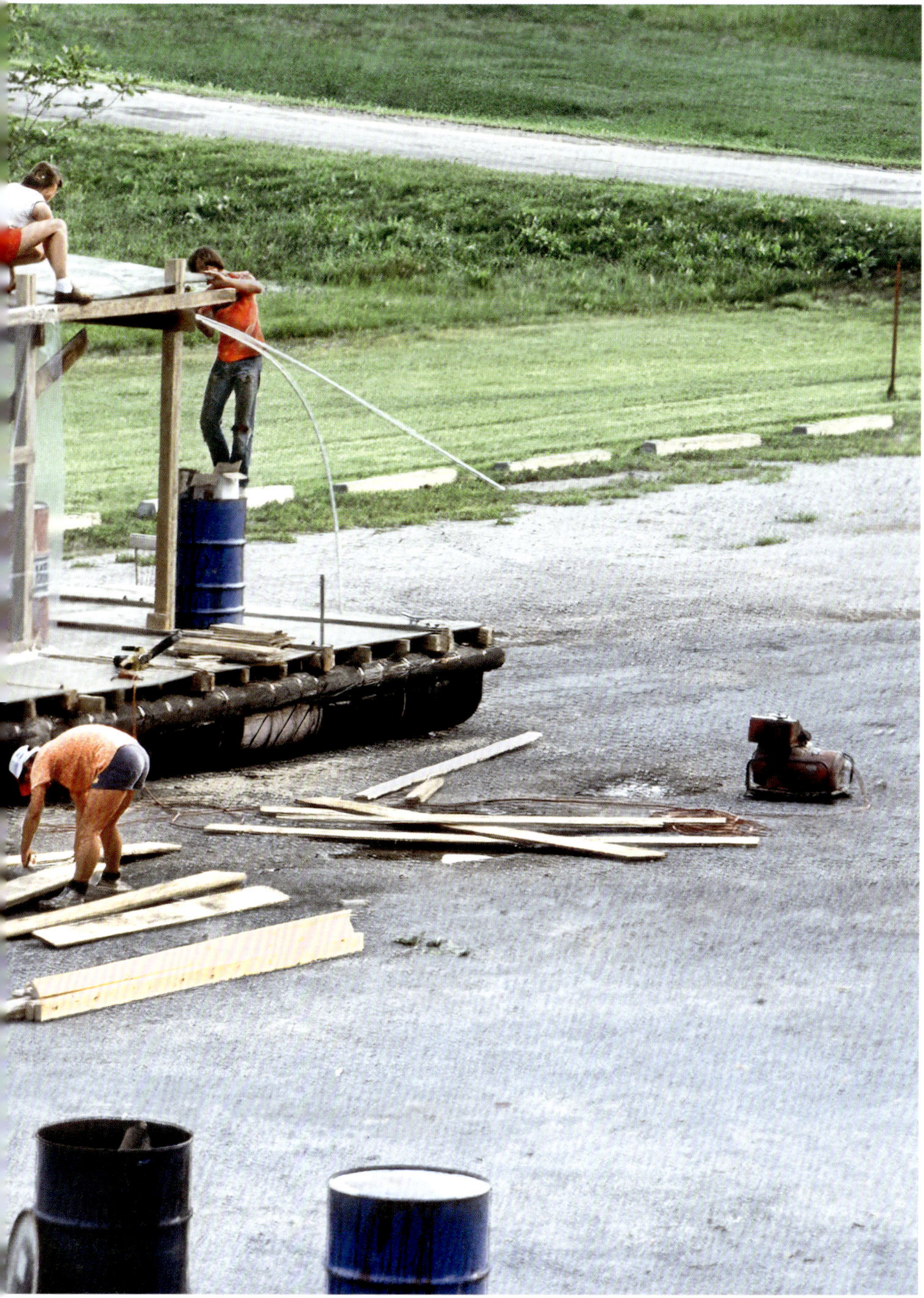

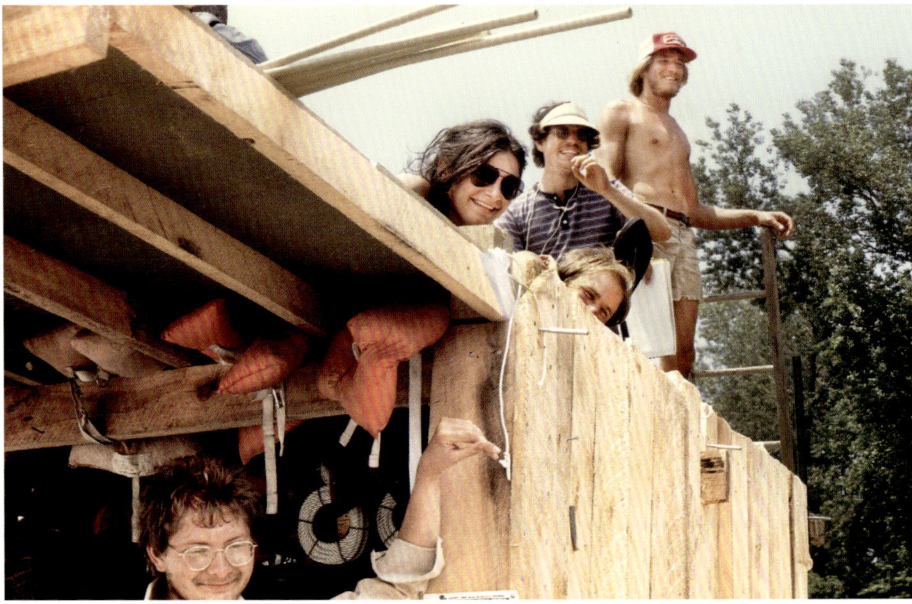

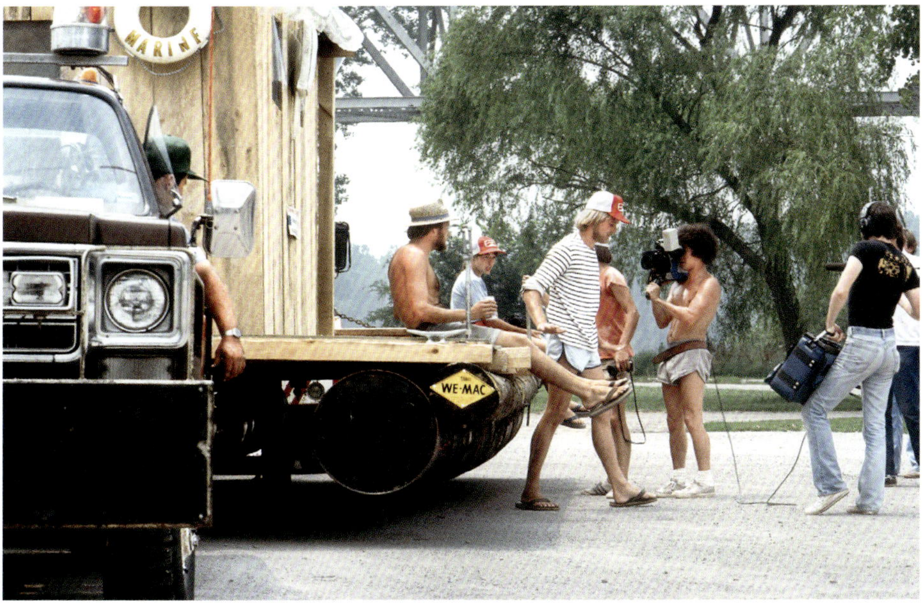
WE-MAC

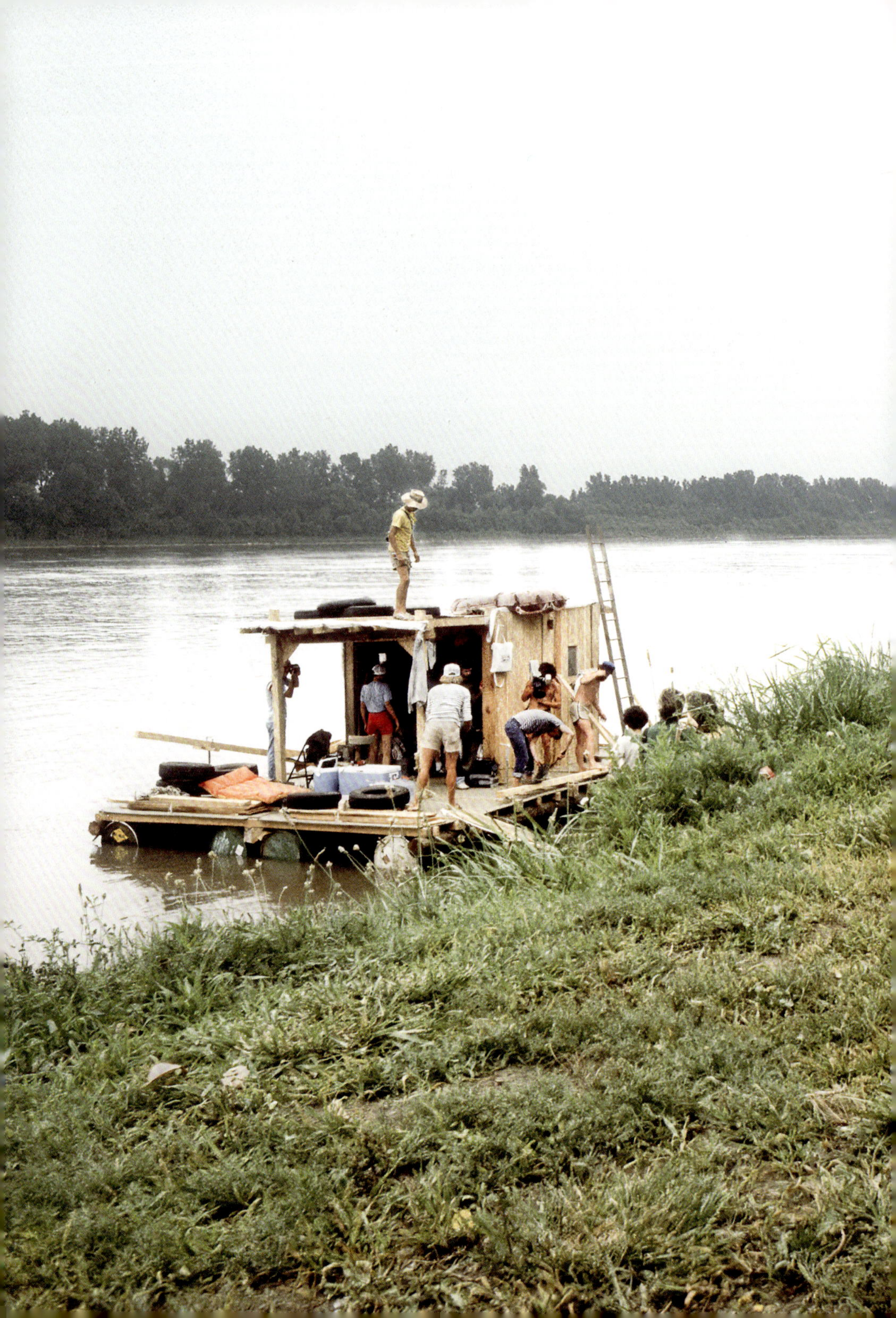

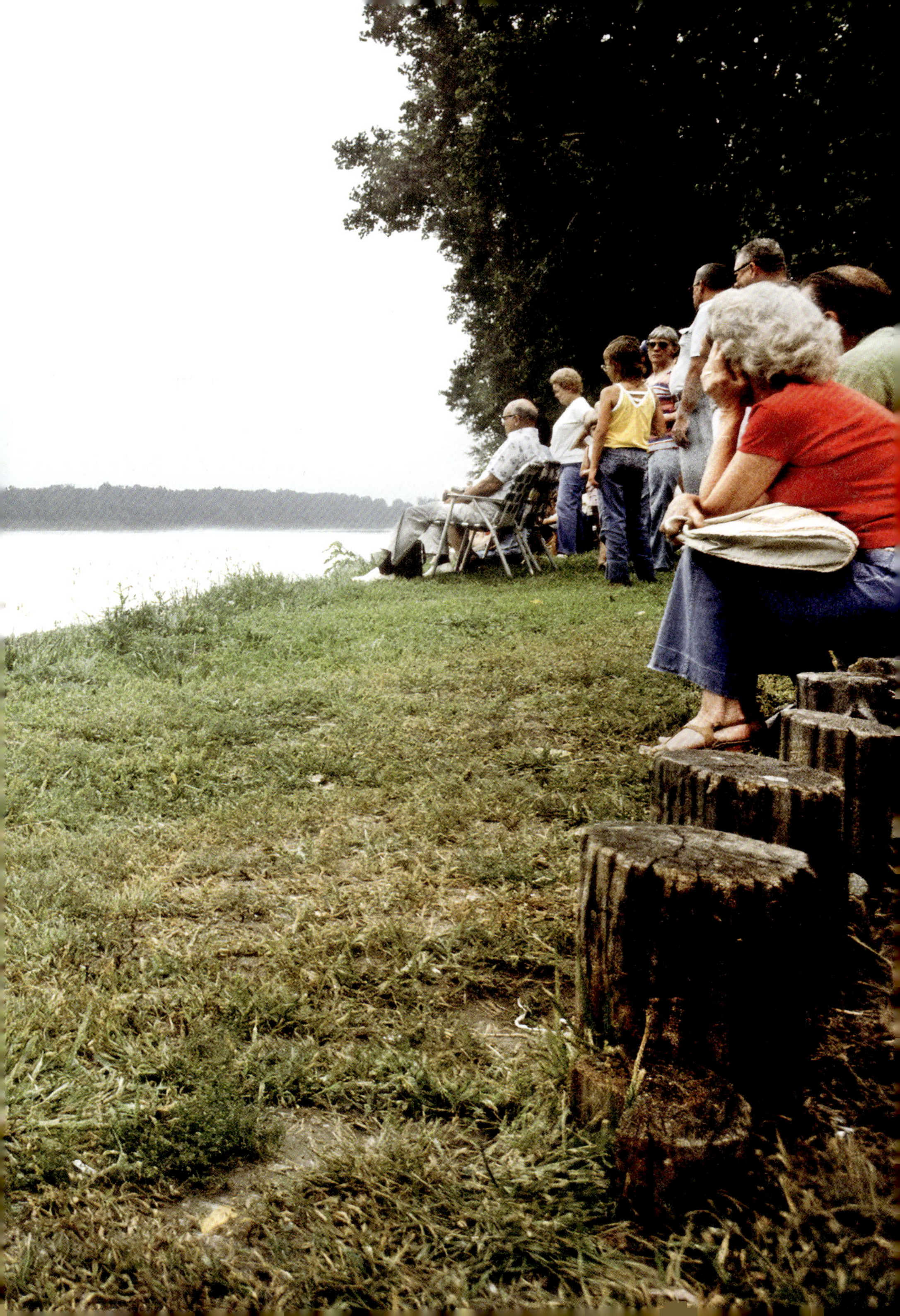

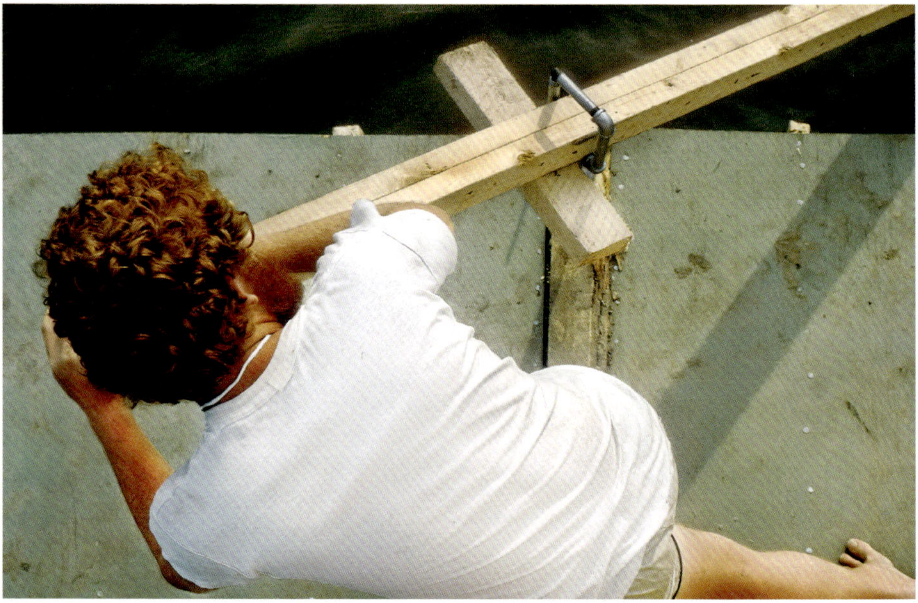

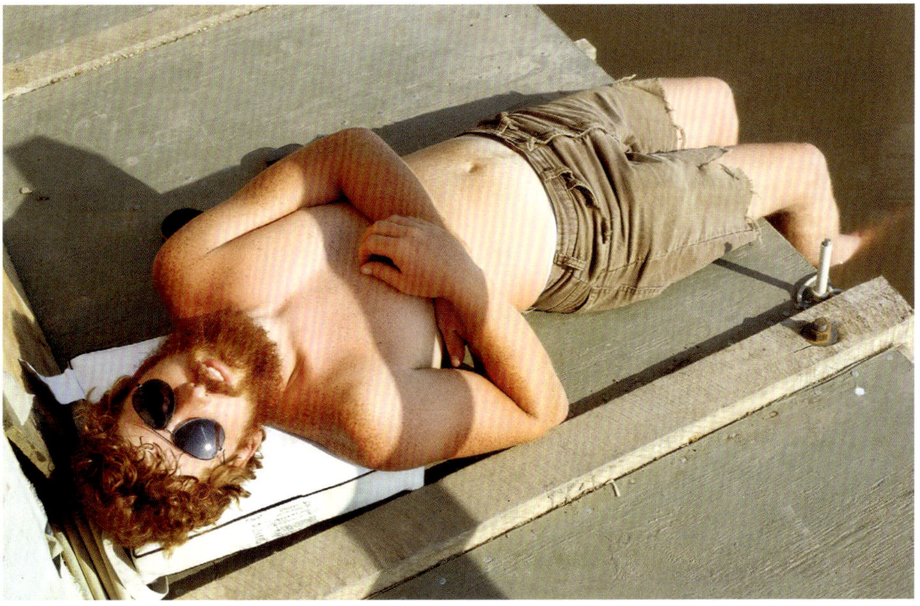

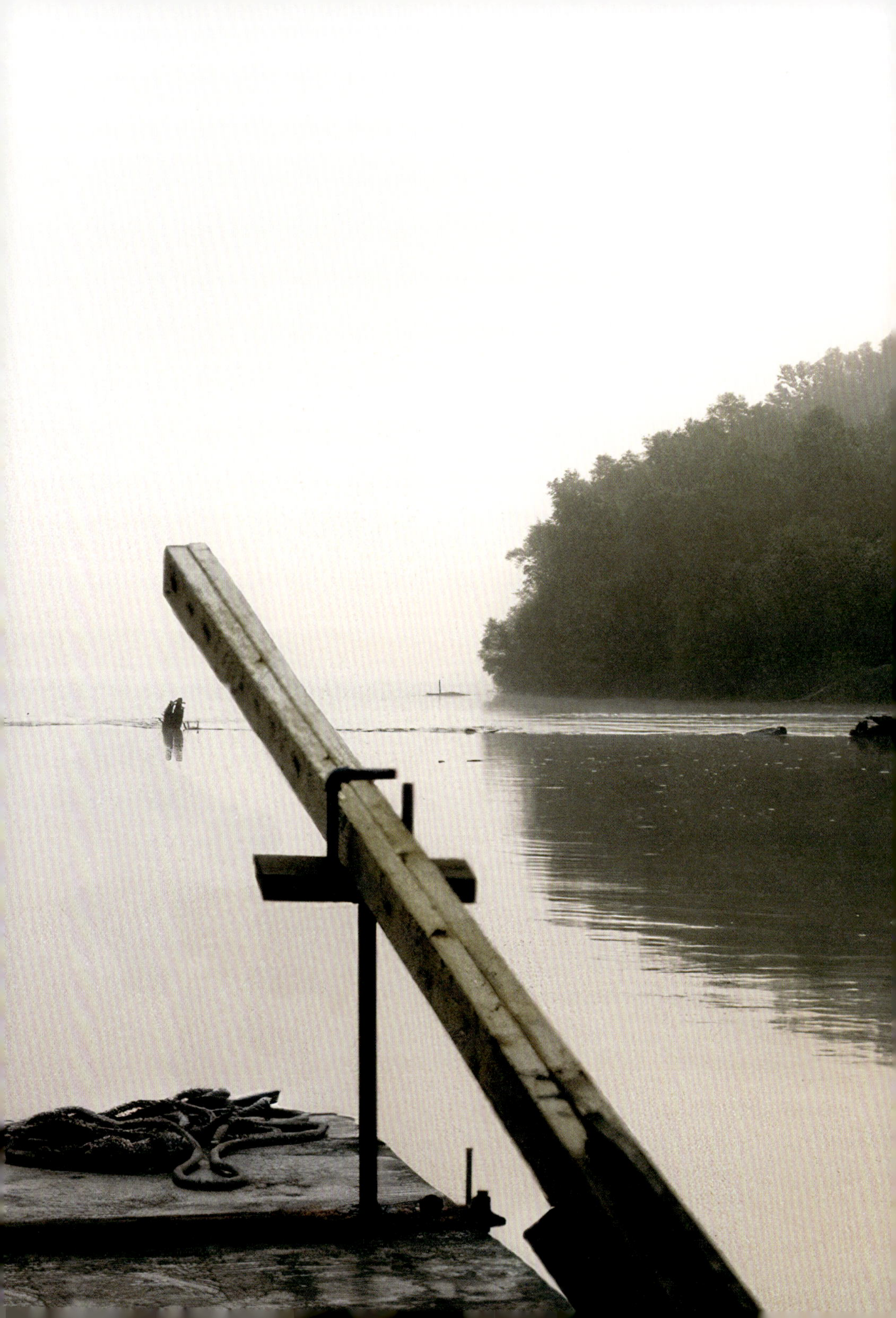

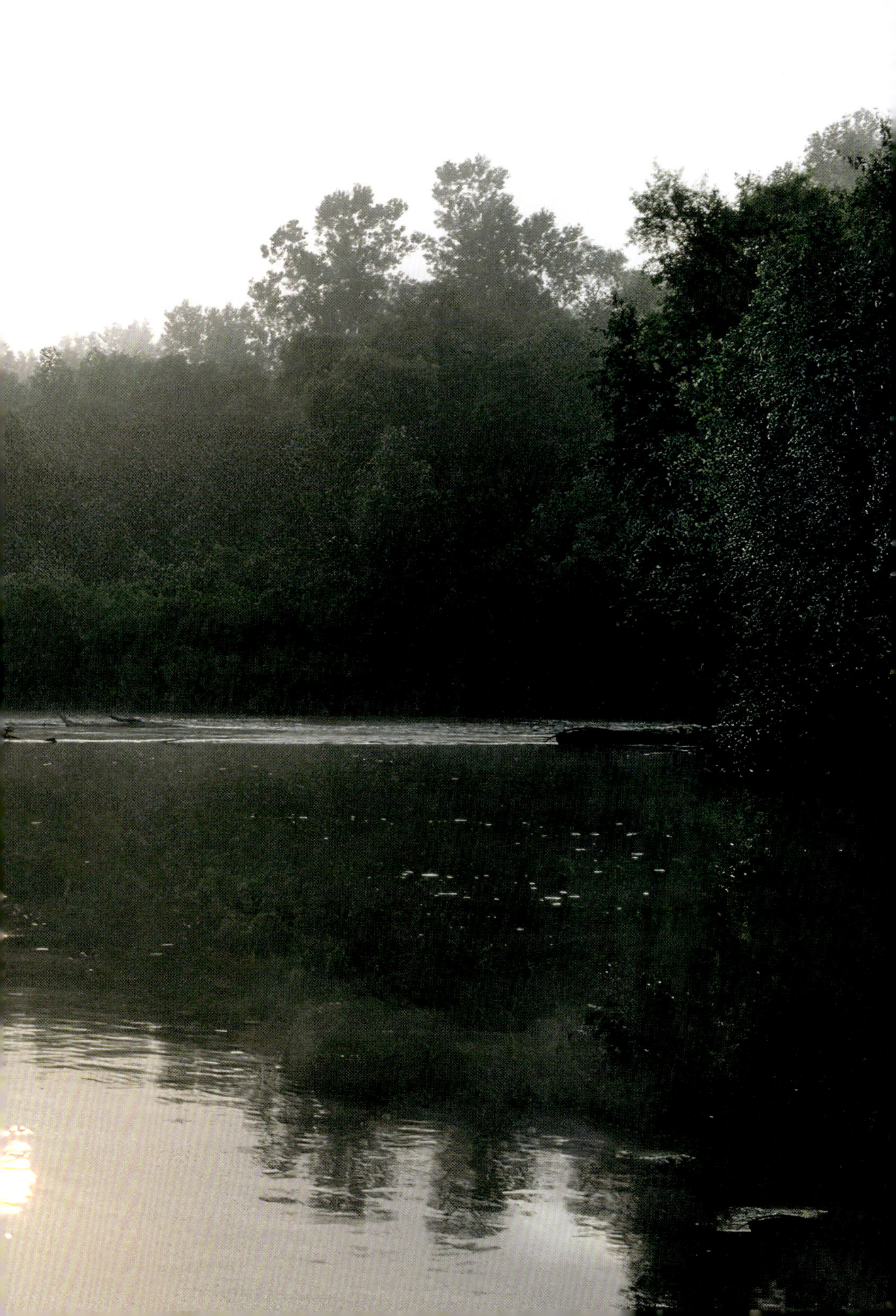

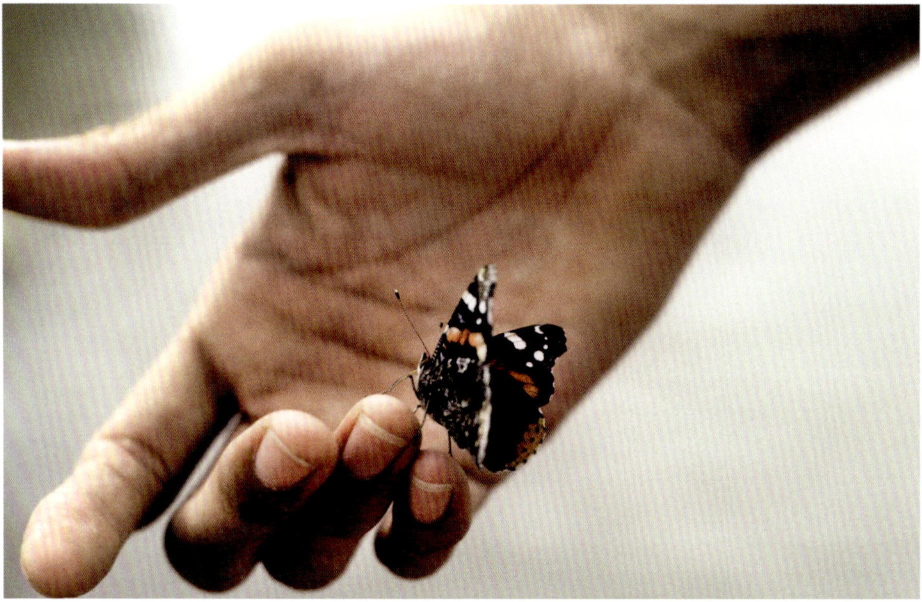

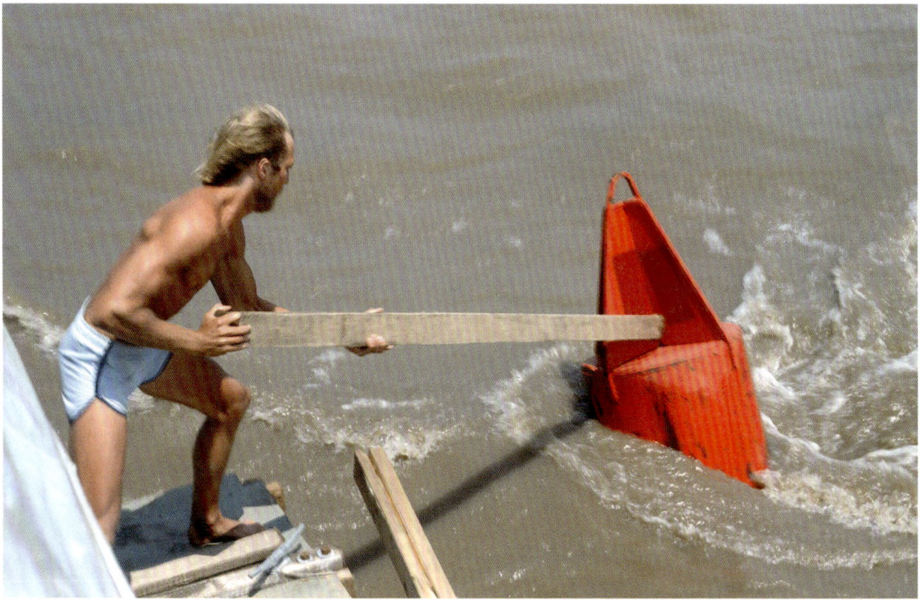

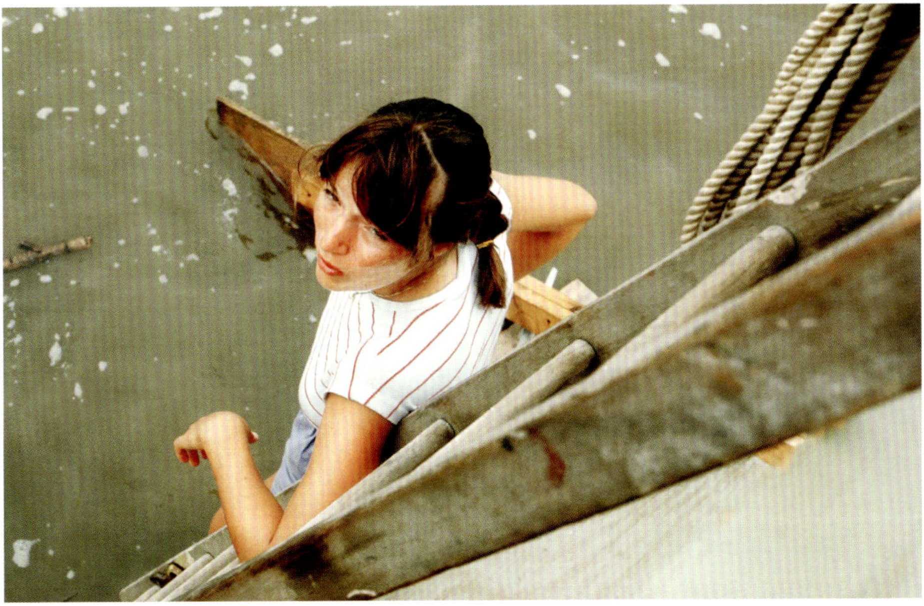

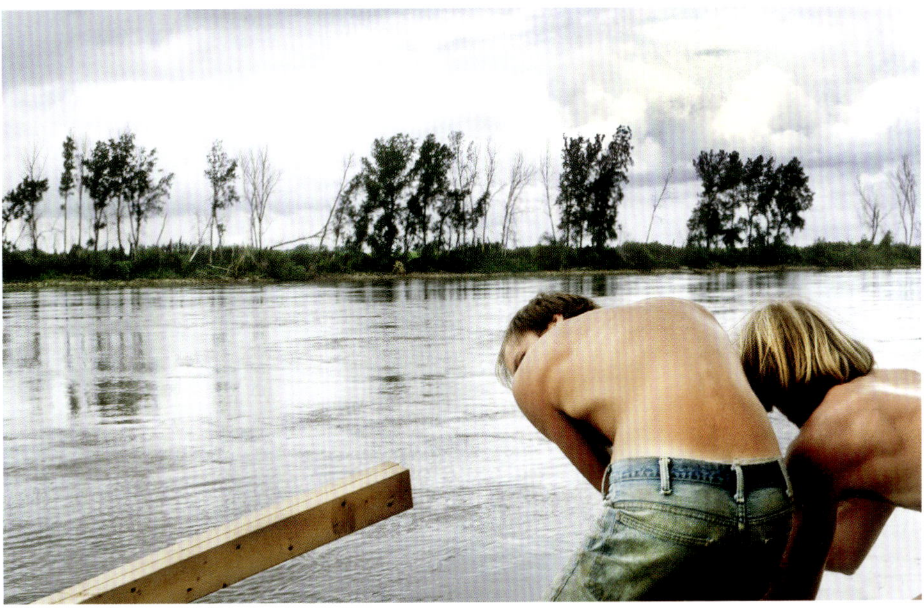

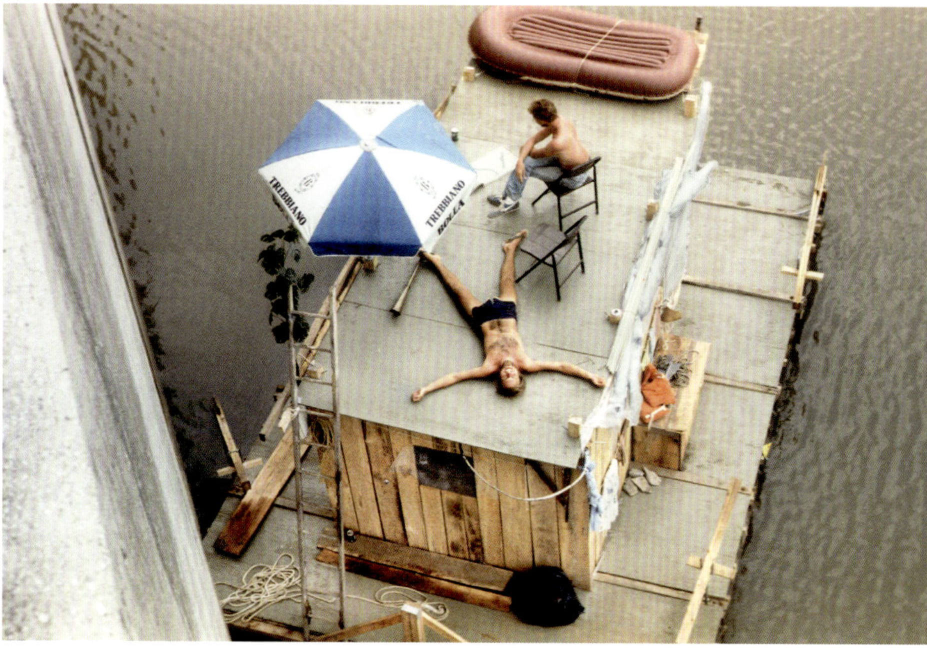
TREBBIANO
TREBBIANO
BOLLA

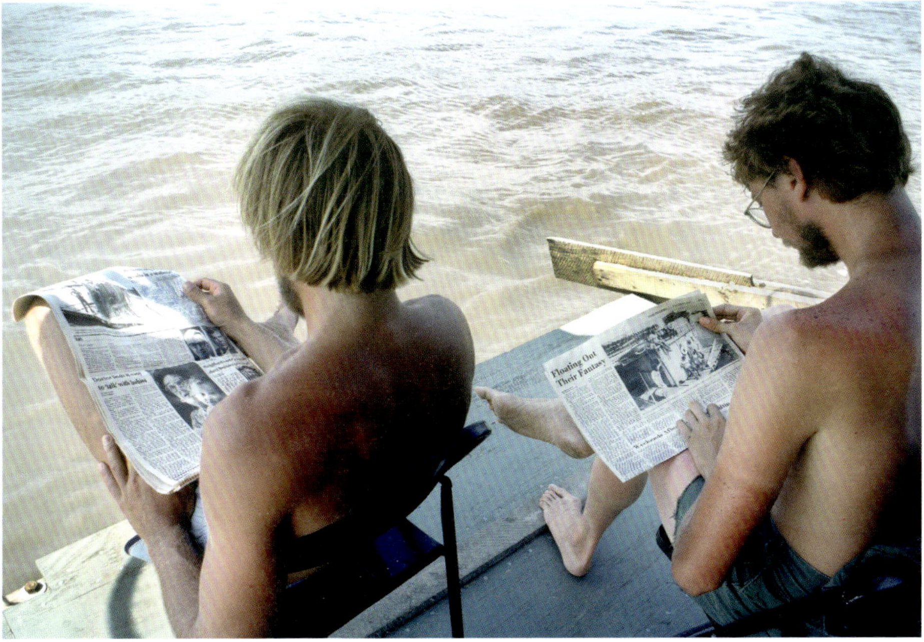
Floating Out
Their Fantasy

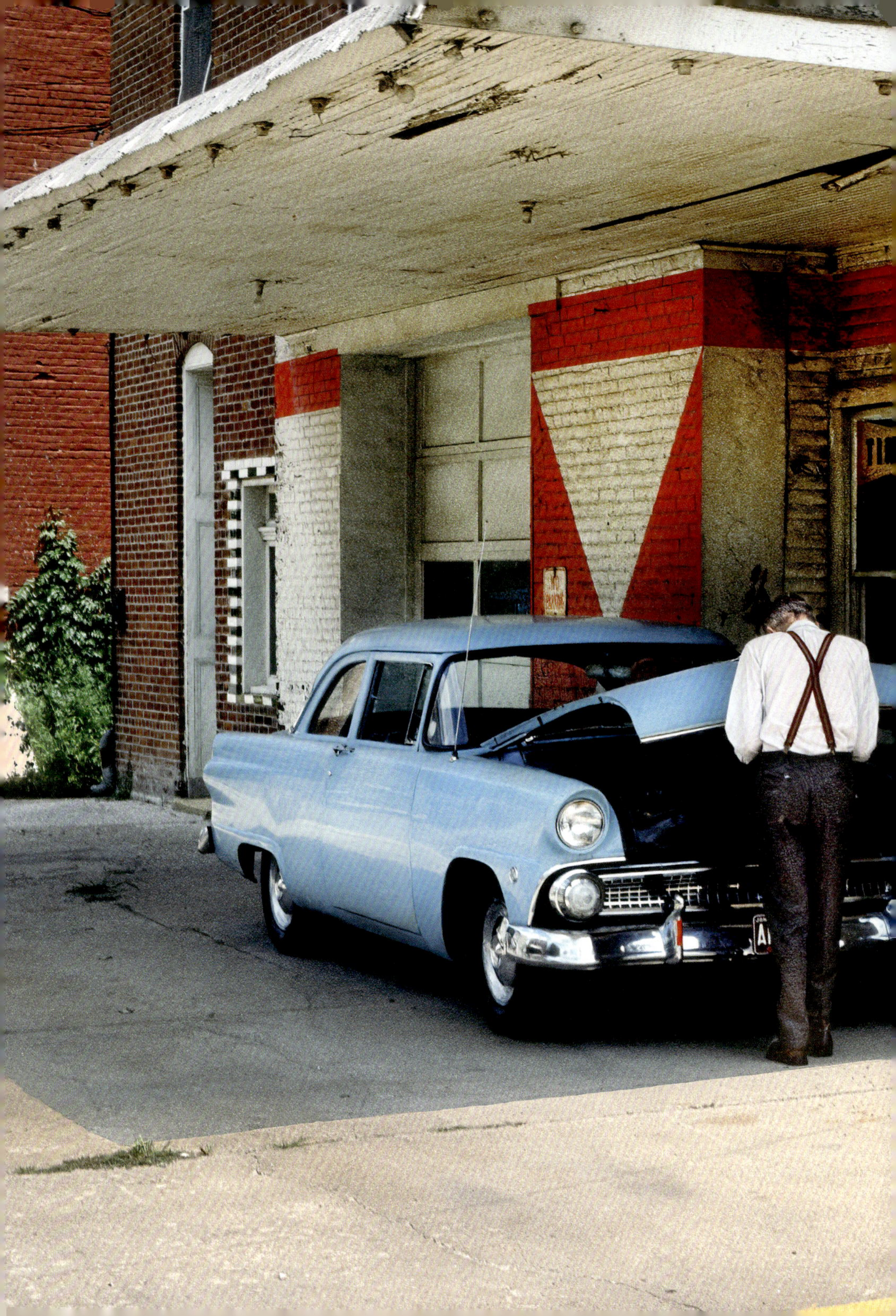

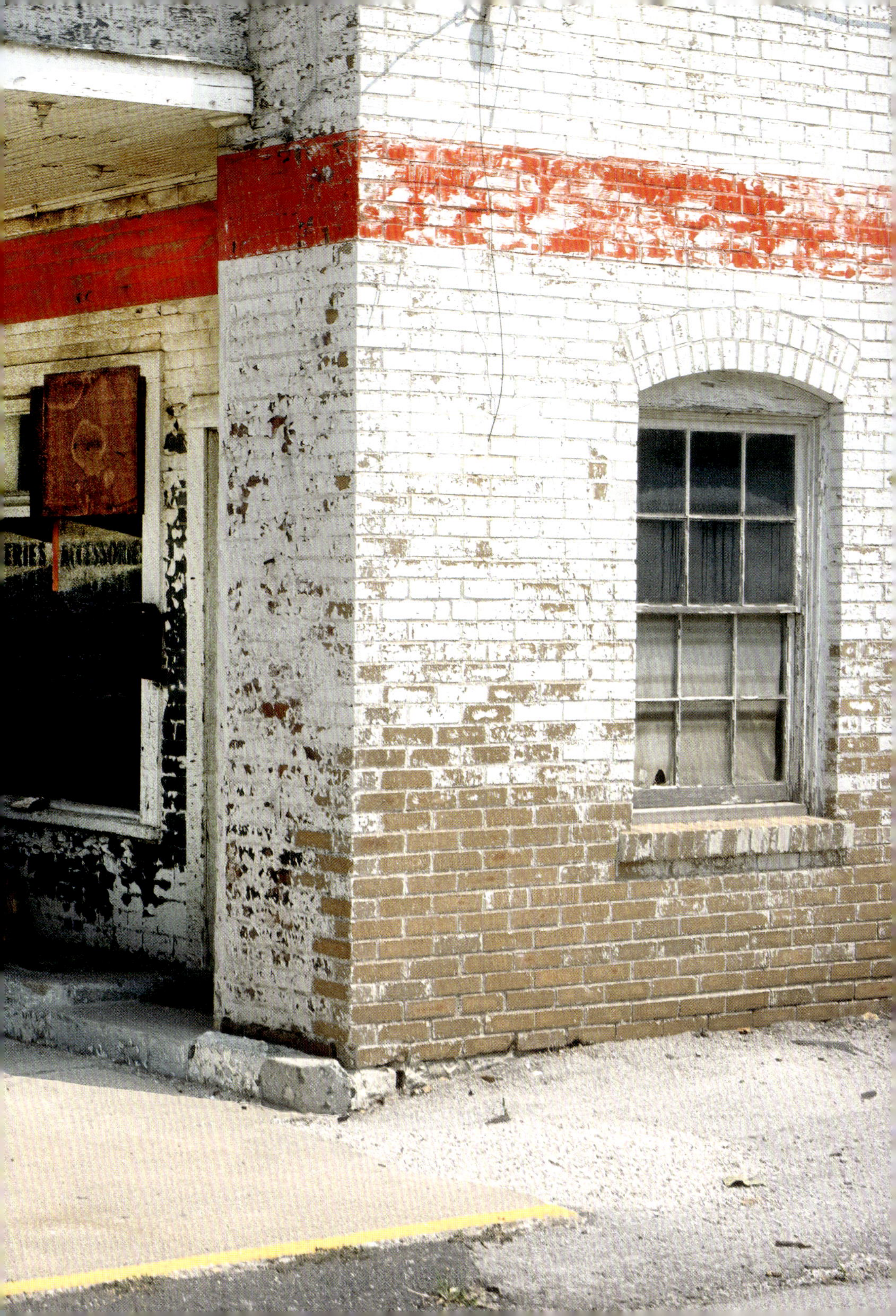

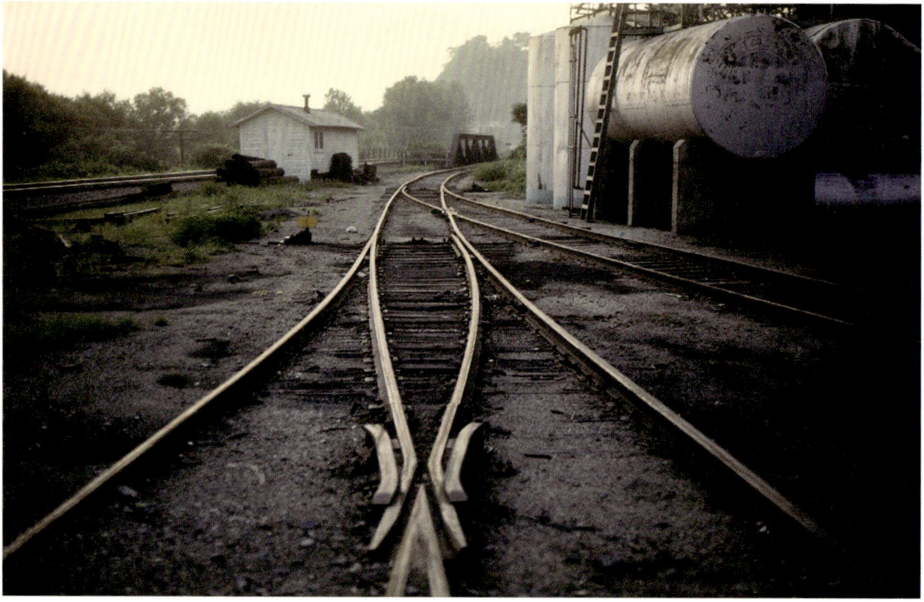

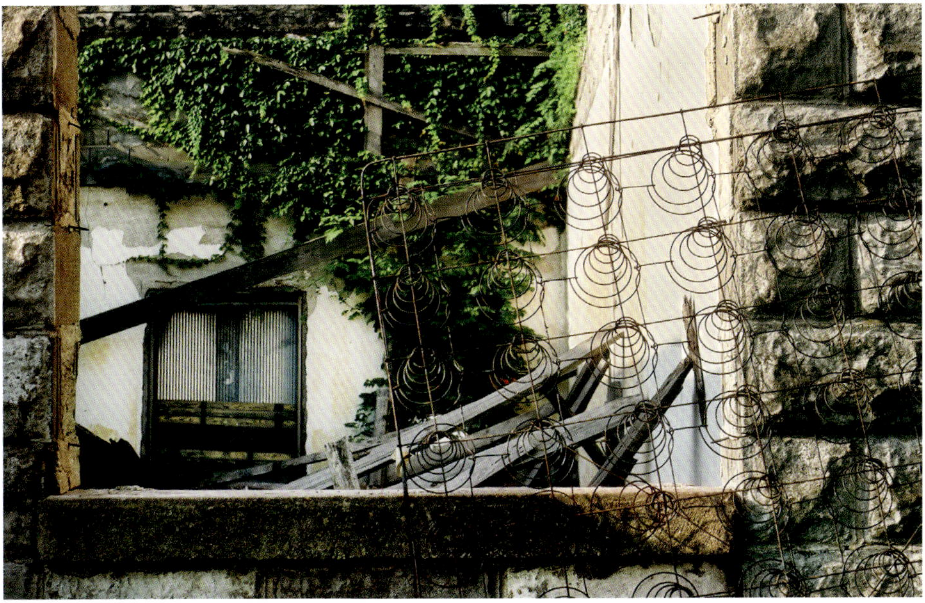

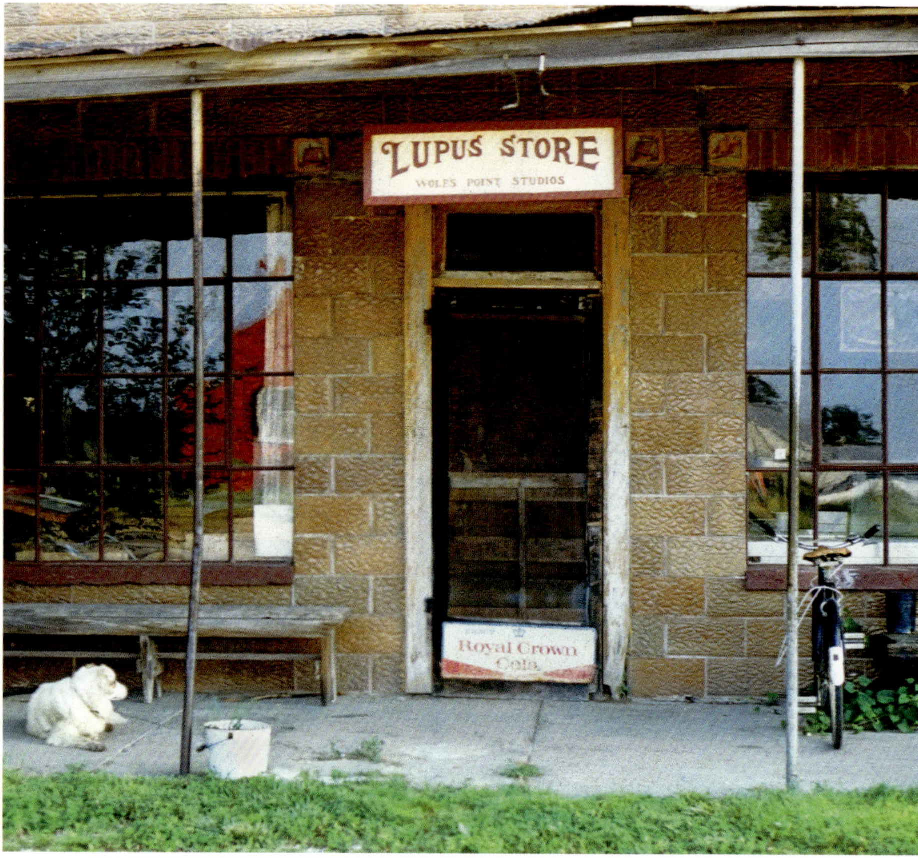

Lupus, Missouri (population 50, give or take). Doug Elley was the city manager and owner of the general store. Doug and his partner Diane had moved to Lupus four years earlier, buying a house for $800 with the notion of revitalizing the town.

Diane worked as a scientific glassblower and pottery instructor at the University of Missouri at Columbia. Doug made stained glass, among other things.

Lupus had a modern two-story, solar-powered outhouse sitting in the middle of town because Doug put it there. He had designed and built it himself with a $1,200 grant from the U.S. Environmental Protection Agency. Doug's Skycrapper was a forward-thinking public convenience that turned human waste into odorless compost within thirty days, with the application of sawdust after each "deposit" and exposure to sunlight in the first-story collection bin.

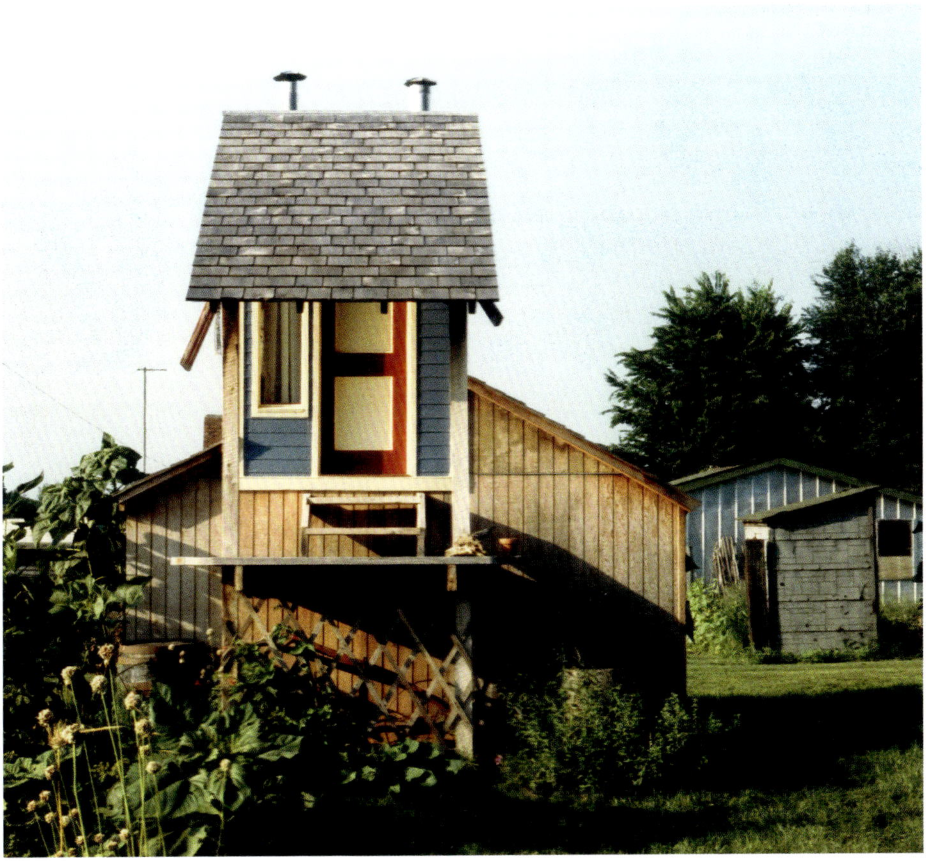

Sunlight also kept the second-story throne room warm in winter. Doug conceived this innovative outhouse for use by settlements along the Missouri River to prevent human waste from entering the river and to reduce the amount of purified river water used by conventional flush toilets.

U.S. Senator William Proxmire saw fit to present Doug's Skycrapper with his notorious Golden Fleece Award in December 1979 for being the most ridiculous expenditure of federal funds that month. Doug was unbowed, declaring upon completing his project on April 4, 1981:

"I hereby dedicate this toilet to the bountiful blessing of waters above and below the surface of our land."

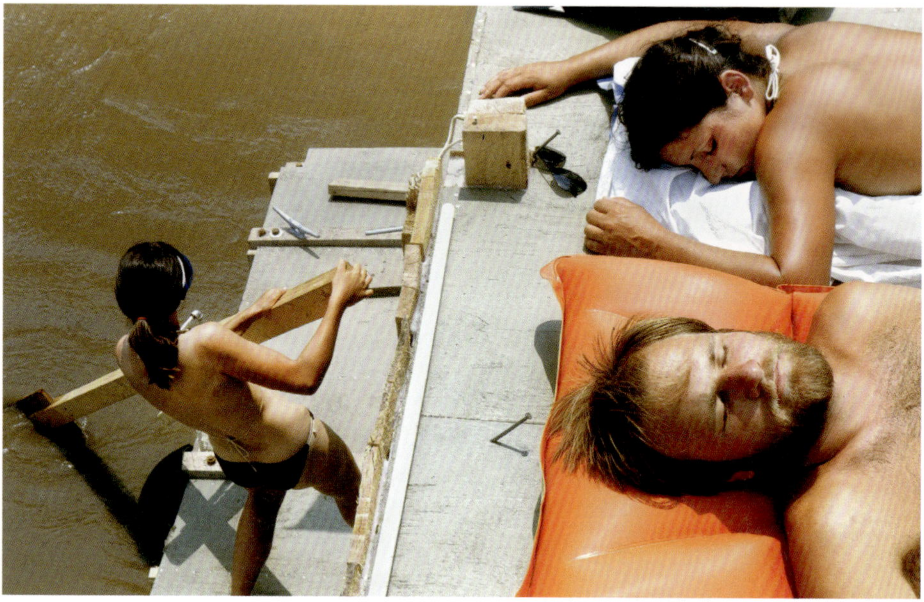

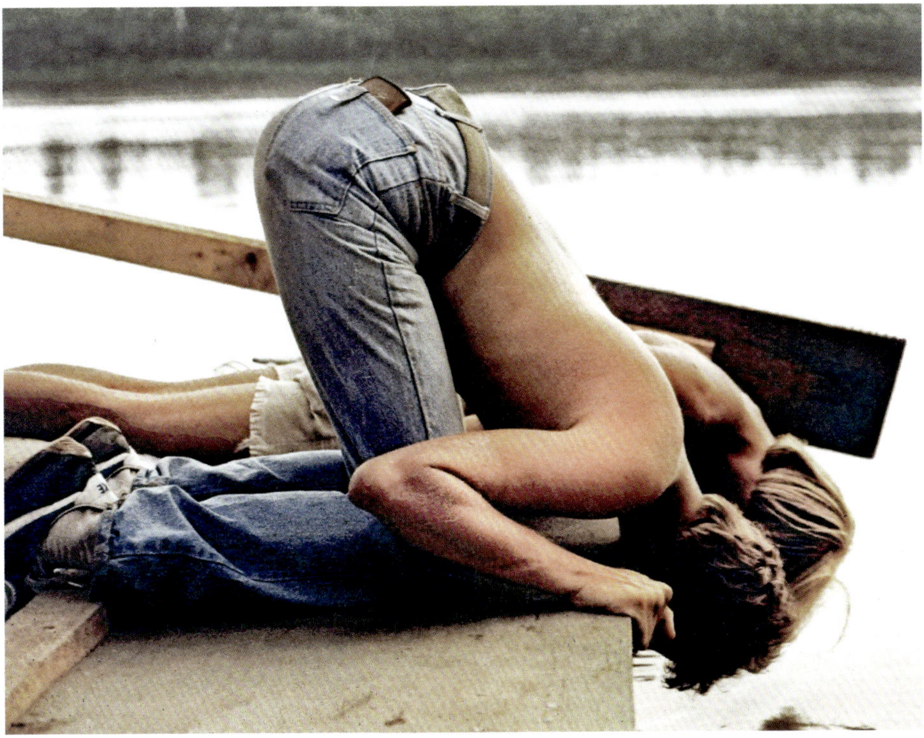

Tom and I check to see if we are sinking. The raft had run over a partially submerged wing dike, and we were worried that one or more of our oil drums had been punctured. The raft seemed to be riding lower in the water on that corner, but it turned out that this was because we were all standing on that corner, looking to see if we were sinking. This is what physicists call the observer effect.

From Ed's Journal:

I met Val Pierce … through Doug's friend Dave. We all met at the tractor pulling contest and got to know each other. Val is a migrant worker/commercial fisherwoman. She … comes from Michigan, California, and Florida. One hell of a person. At one point in her life she was a shepherdess in Switzerland. She plans on moving back to California in August. She chews her words, has large hands, is very kind, sensitive and considers Nabokov her favorite author. She has great beginnings for laugh wrinkles and she has bags under her eyes. Hard physical work has become her life. I must stress what beautiful hands she has. Her wrists are big and her hands are those of a potato eater in one of Van Gogh's early paintings. She has been working with plants which have been heavily sprayed with insecticide. Her fingers were badly calloused and darkened black from working with them. I've never met anyone with such a good attitude about life … I may never see her again.

Ed then writes the lyrics of George Gershwin's "Summertime" into his journal.

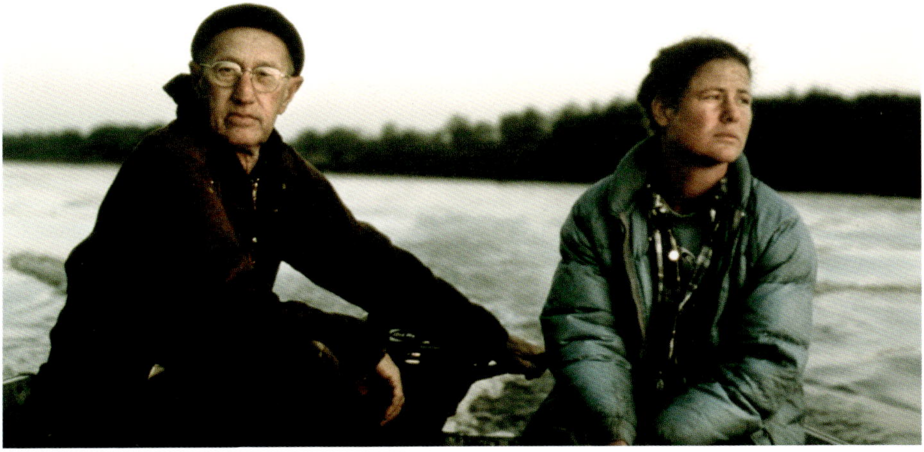

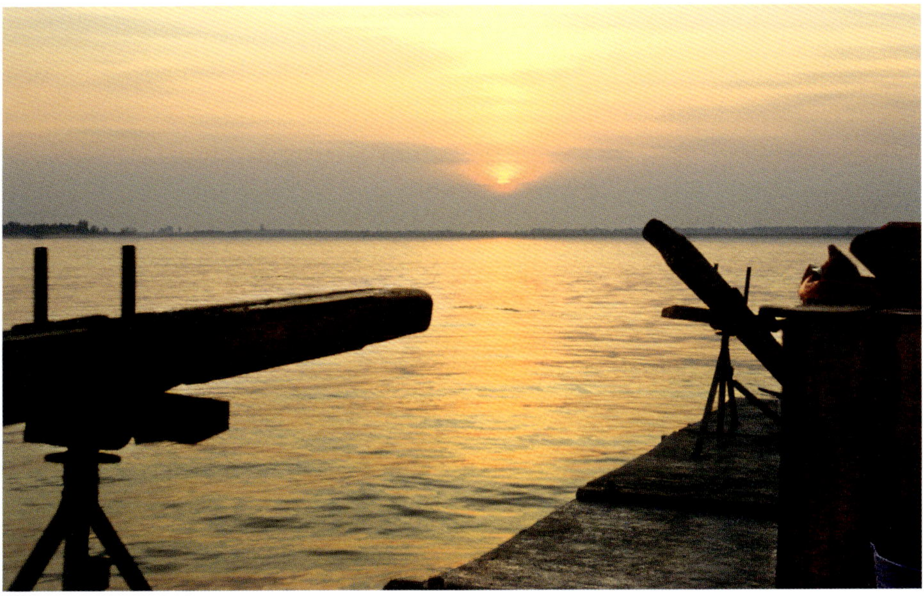

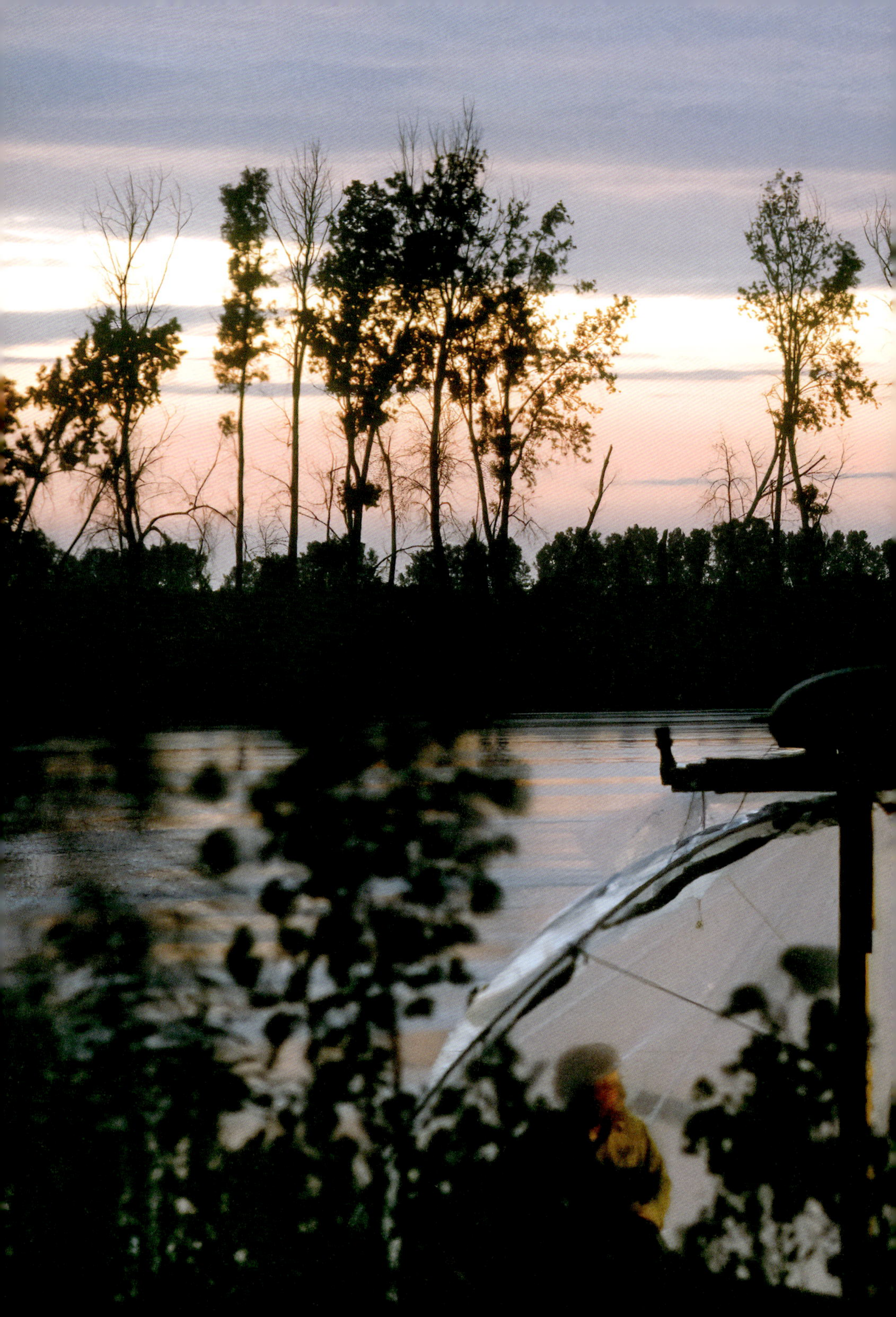

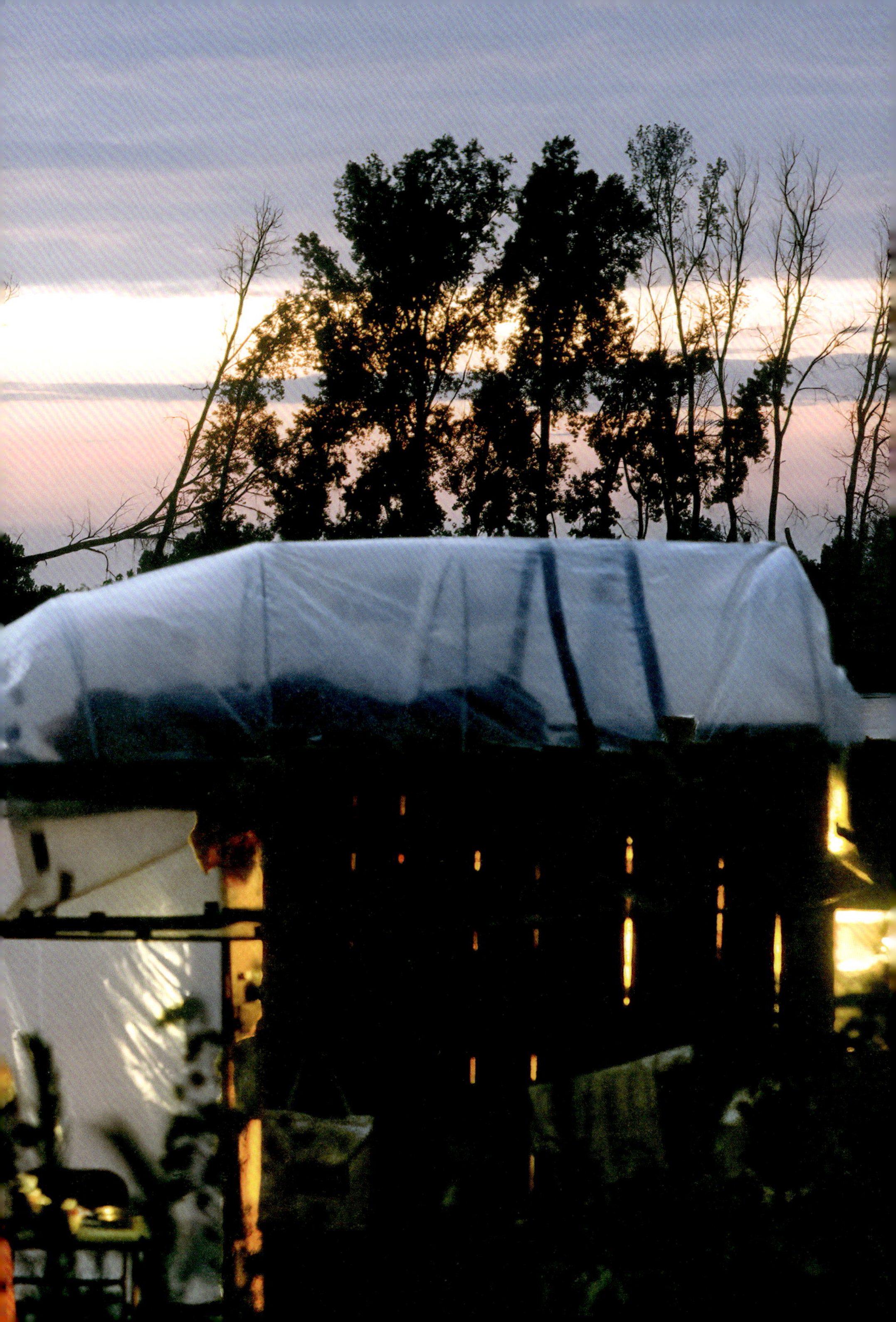

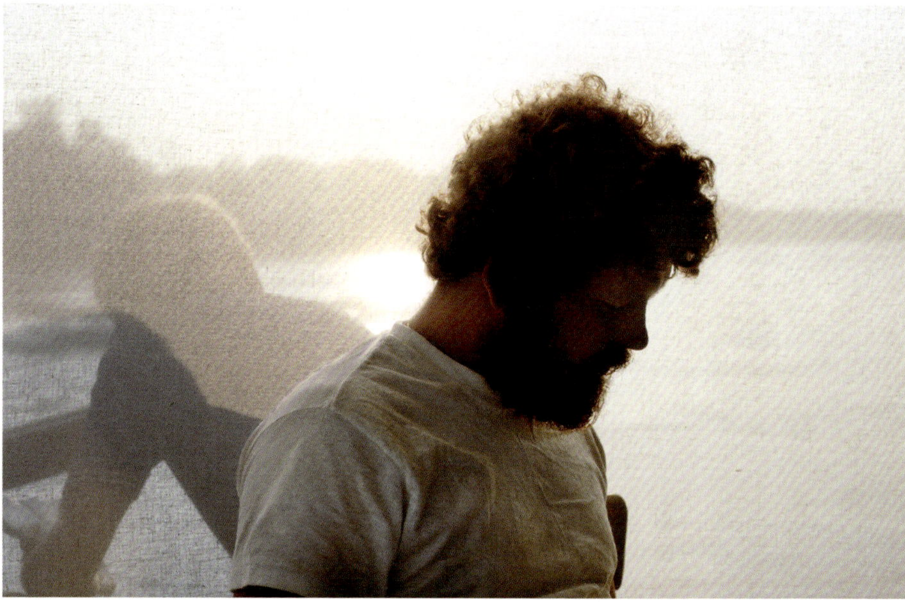

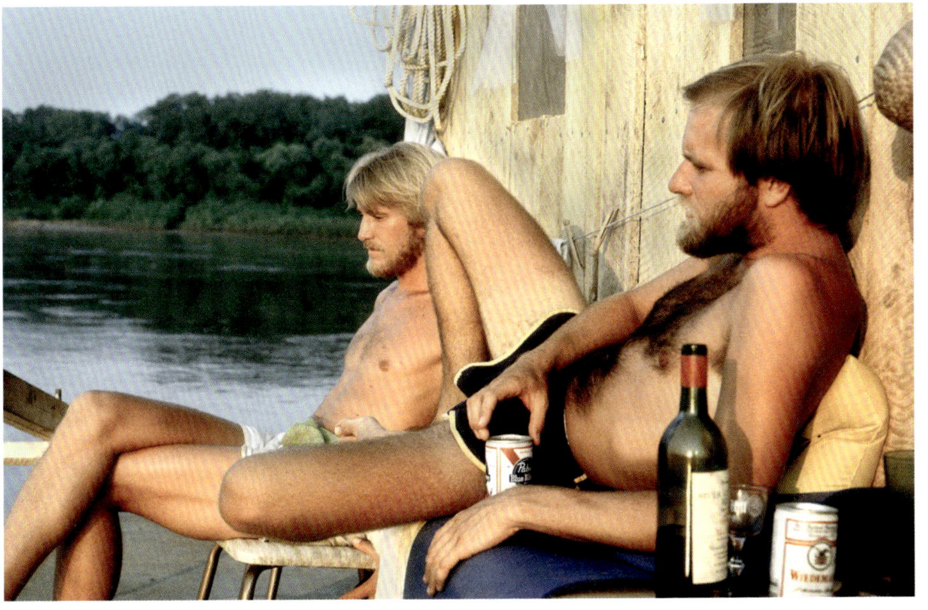

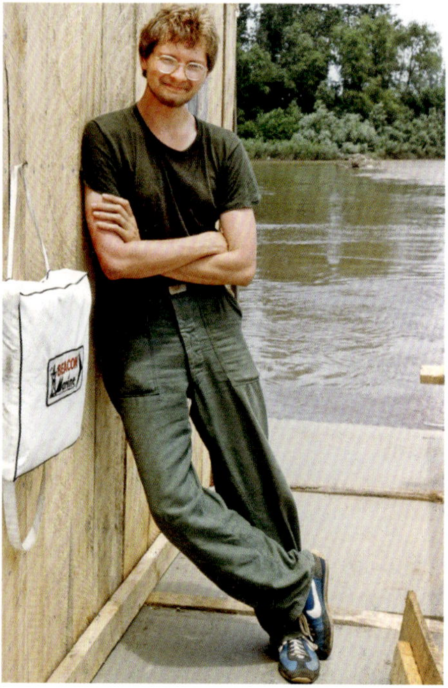
BEACON

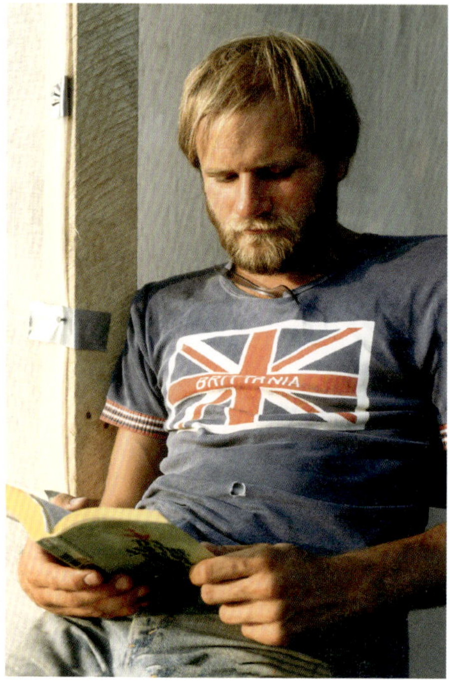
BRITTANIA

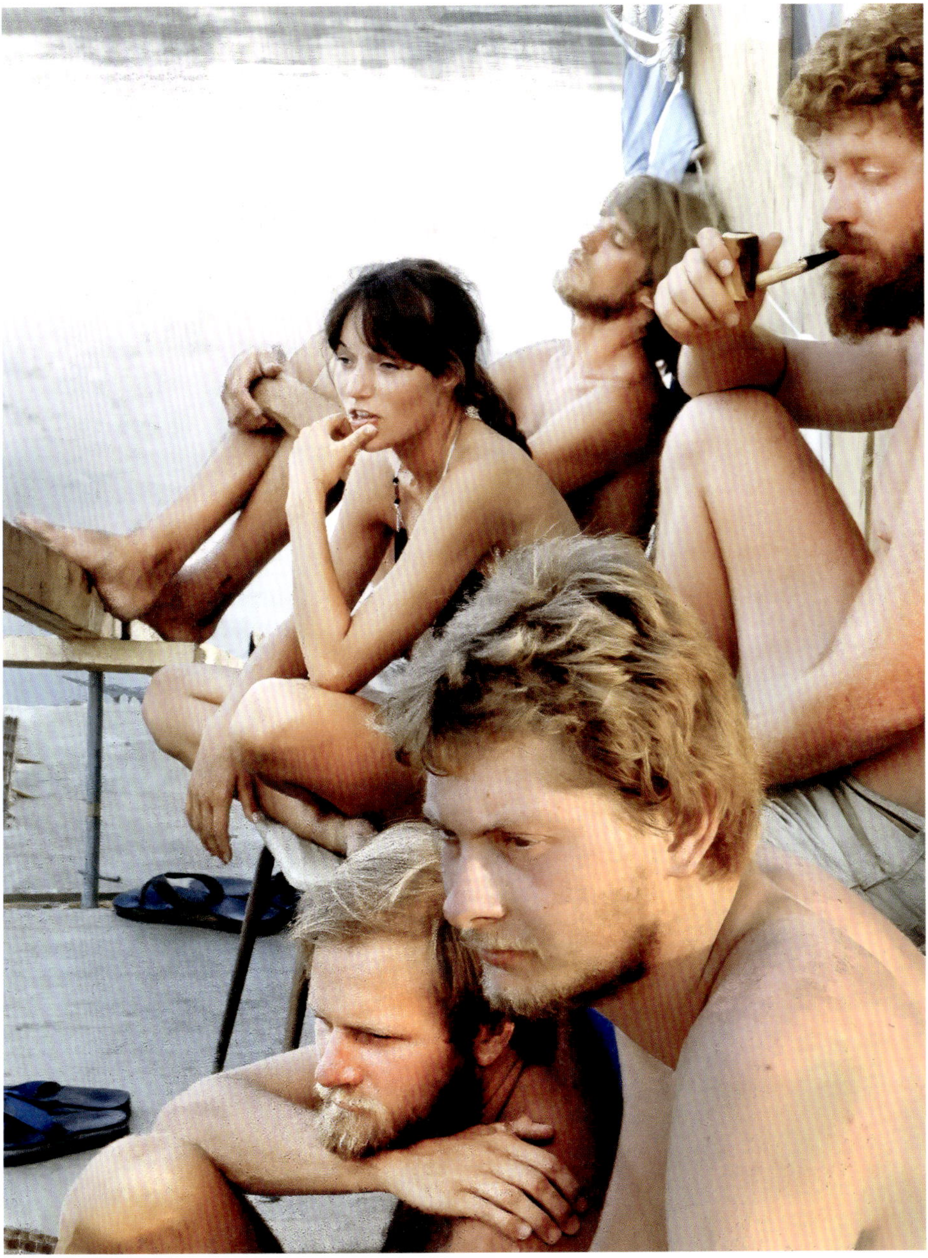

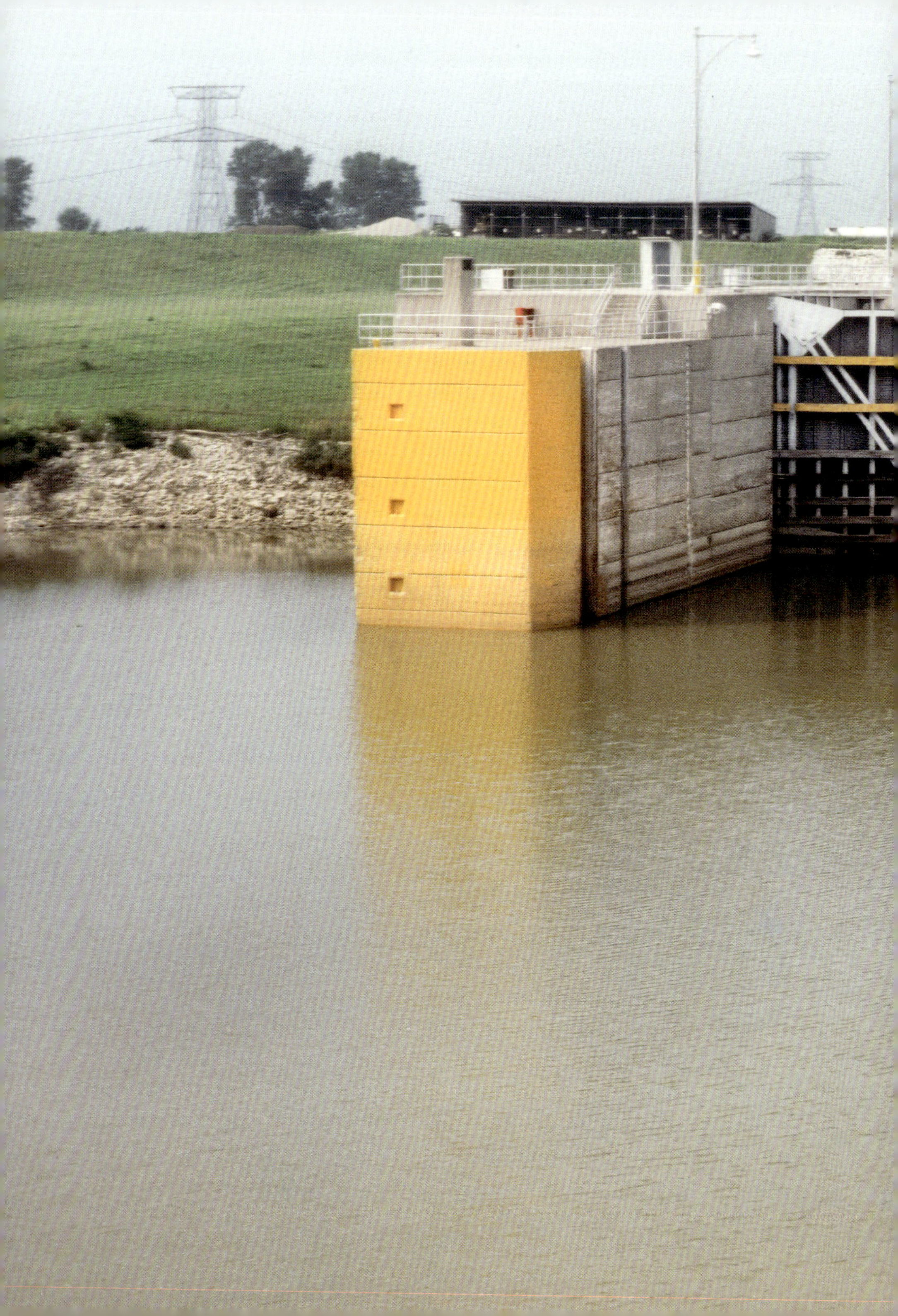

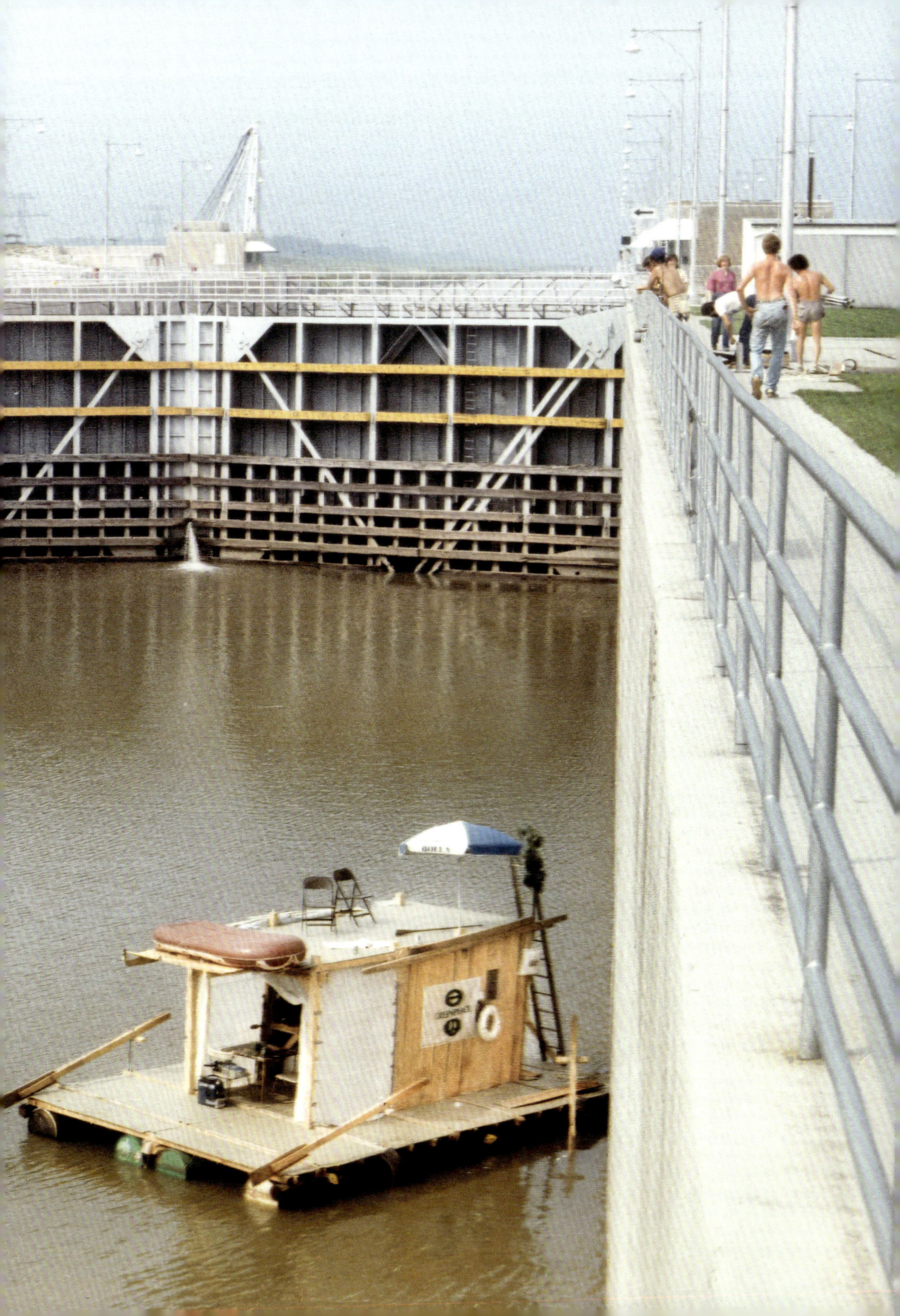

The Chain of Rocks Canal is an eight-and-a-half-mile-long artificial waterway that connects the Missouri and the Mississippi Rivers twelve miles north of the St. Louis Gateway Arch. The U.S. Army Corps of Engineers built the canal to bypass a dangerously shallow section of the Mississippi River immediately north of St. Louis. A limestone ledge left behind during the last ice age, aptly named the Chain of Rocks, juts up out of the riverbed there, resulting in a shallow draft that can be dangerous for even small craft.

Maneuvering through the Chain of Rocks would have meant running a substantial risk of hanging our raft up on the rocks and even capsizing. We chose instead to pass through the canal and its eight and a half miles of water with no current, or dead water. Eight miles of dead water is a big obstacle for a two-ton raft with no motor or sail. A crew of six cannot row a raft of that weight eight miles in a reasonable amount of time.

Our plan was to reenact the barge-hauling mule system on the Erie Canal and have selected crew members use ropes to pull the raft through the canal all the way to the Mississippi River. Since none of the crew were actually mules, this methodology turned out to be about as practical as rowing.

We struggled along for a few hundred yards, and then the U.S. Coast Guard showed up.

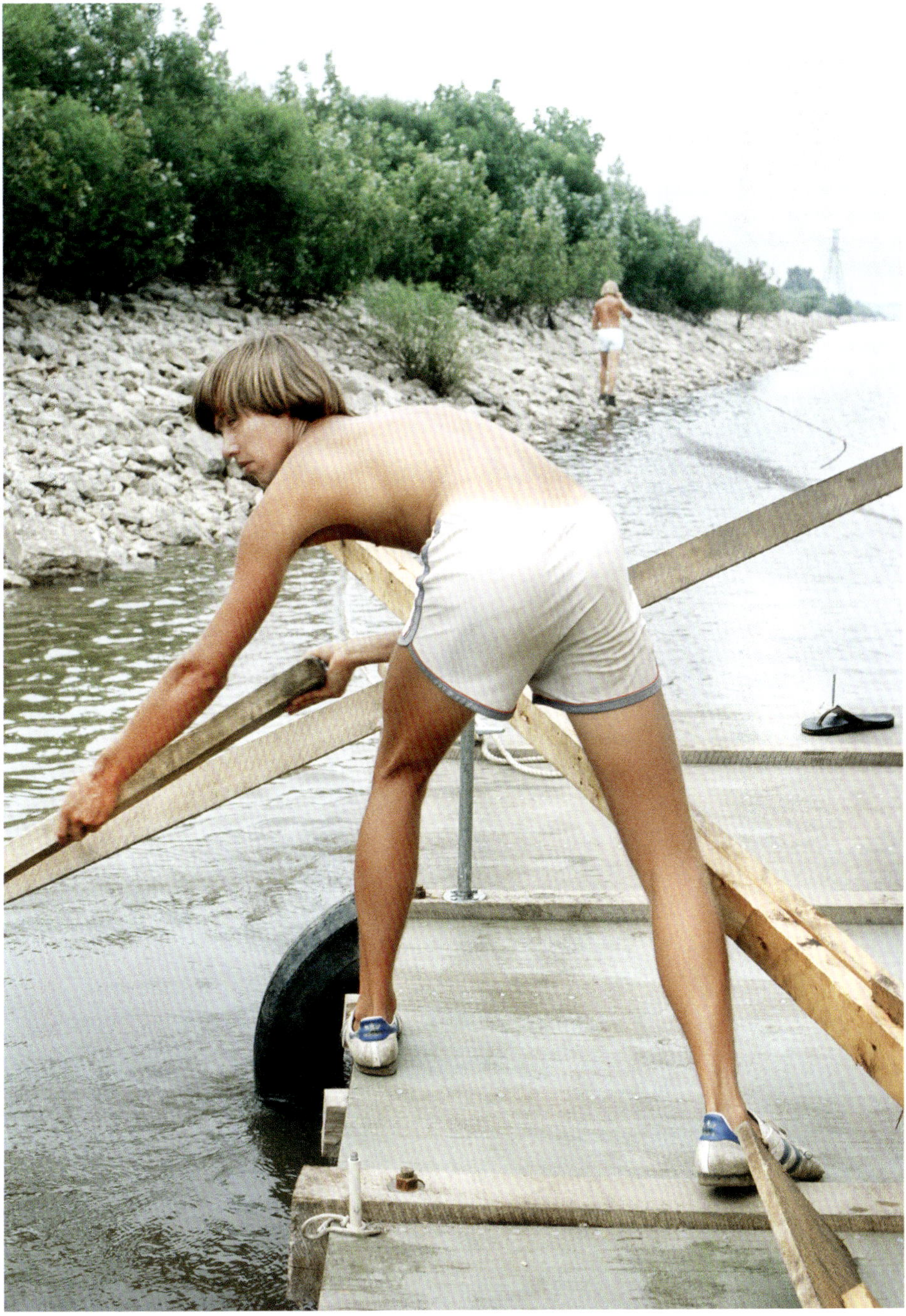

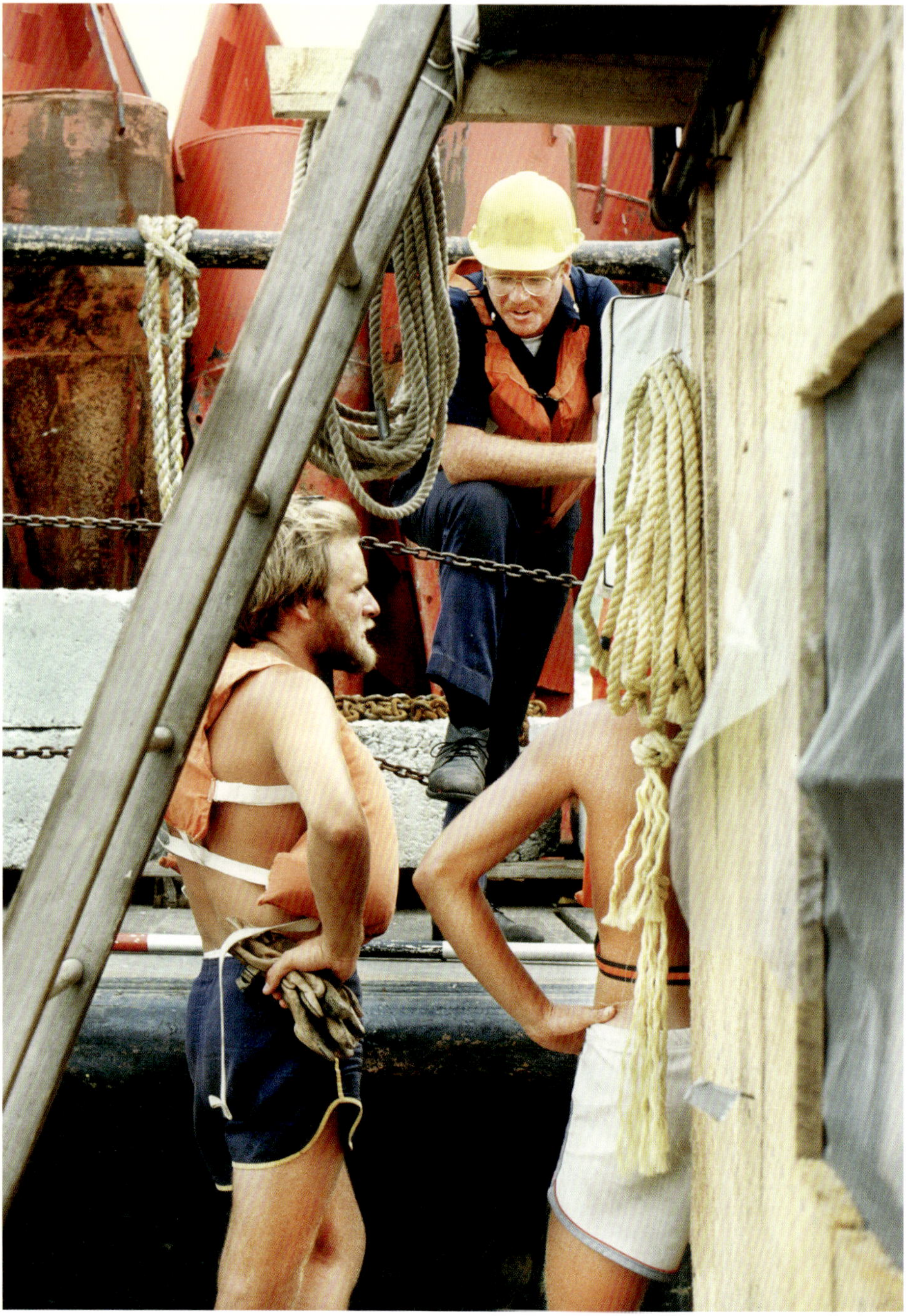

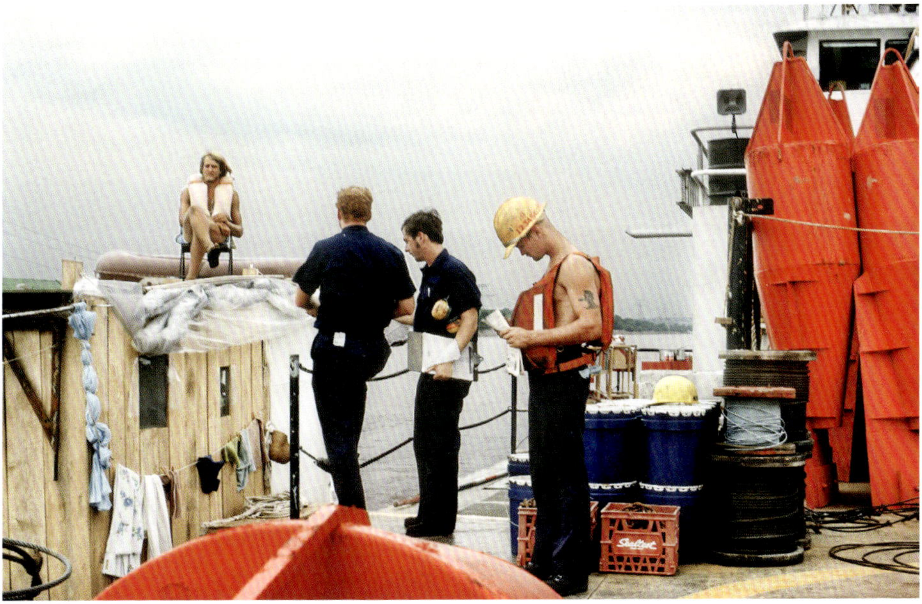
Sealtest

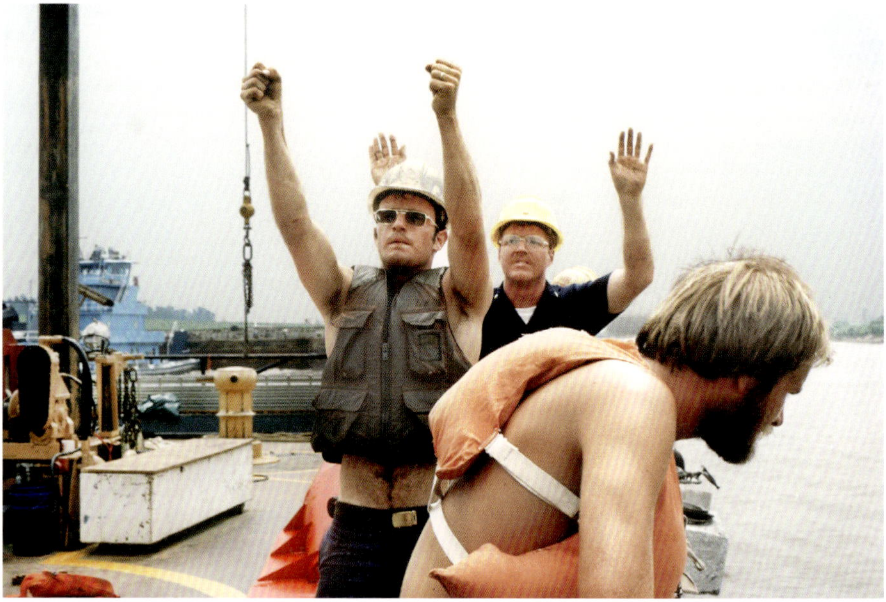

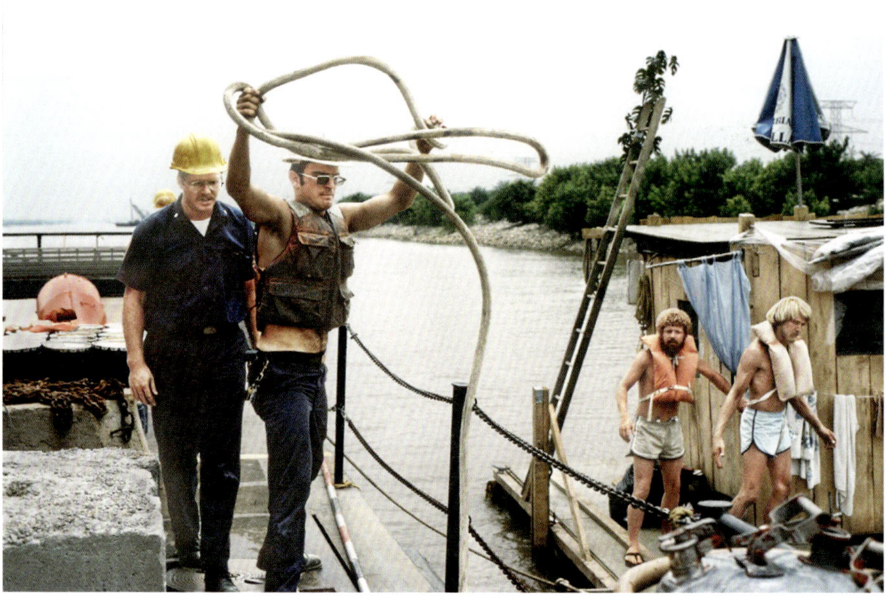

A metal deck cleat was bolted onto each of the four corners of the raft's main deck. We used them to tie the raft off to an object on shore or to our anchor line at night. We needed to tie the raft to the Coast Guard buoy tender so it could tow us the rest of the way through the canal. We wound one end of a rope around two of these cleats and tossed the opposite end to the crew so they could secure it to the deck of their tow. The pilot revved the tow engine, and we started moving forward.

The raft's bow immediately nosed into the water, six inches of which washed over the deck, as we had not designed the raft to move through the water at speed. All that moving water put enormous stress on the raft's deck cleats until one of them was ripped out of its mounting and shot across the deck like a bullet.

No one was hurt.

The crews rerigged the ropes around the forward telephone pole joint on the deck and placed ballast on the back of the raft so it would not nose down into the water.

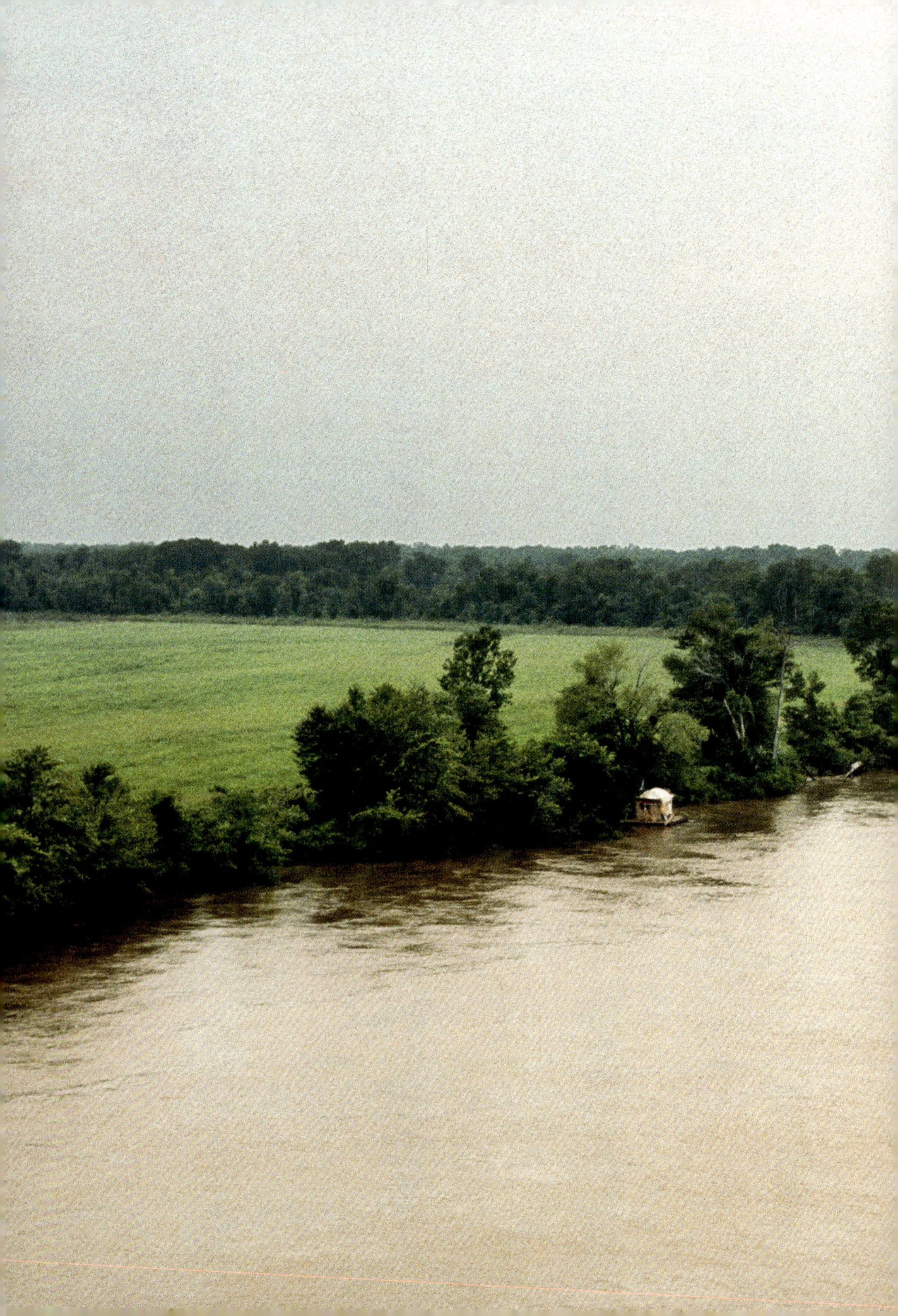

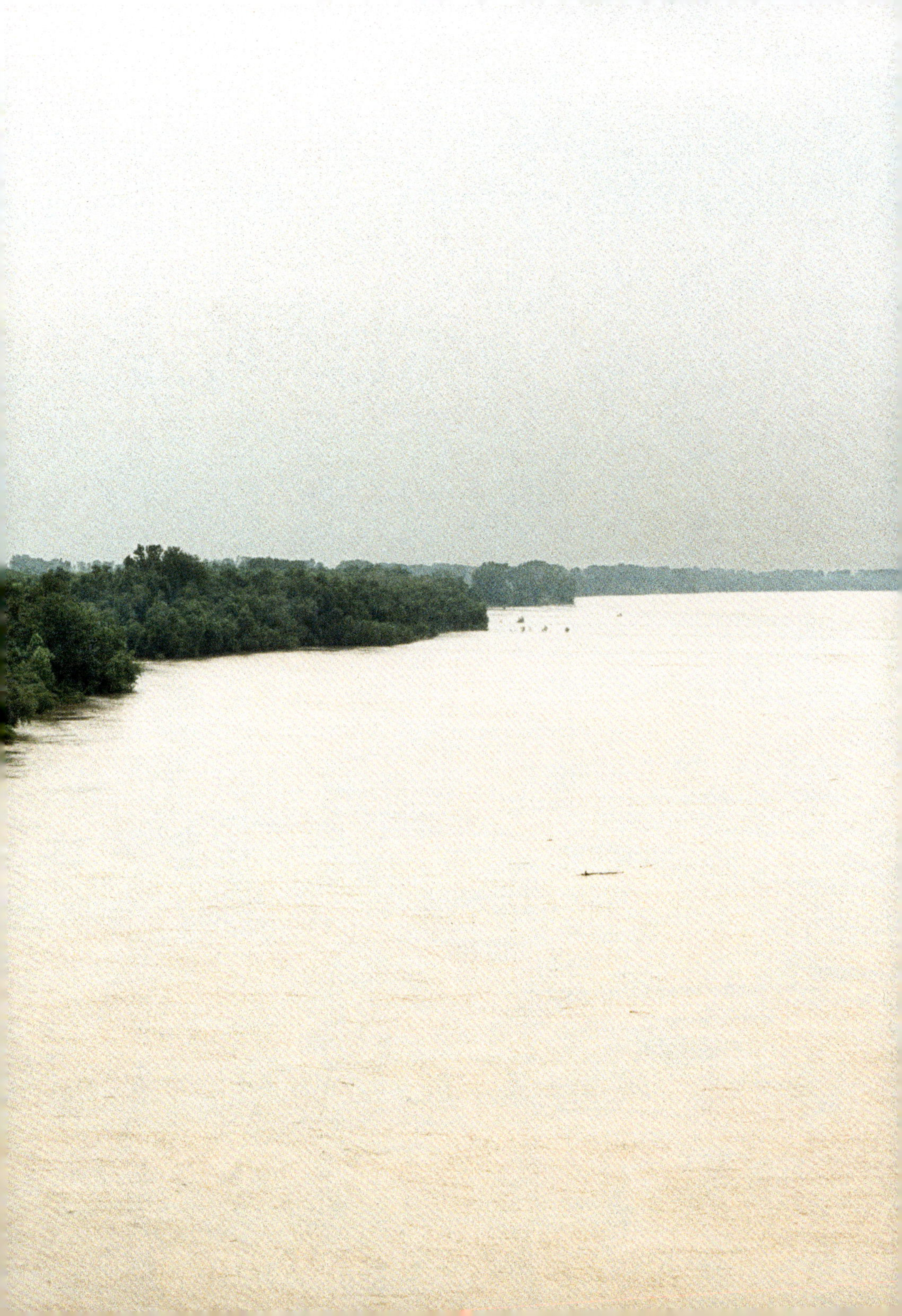

Rick and Cleg had to leave the raft in St. Louis and return to Colorado. After his return home, Cleg recalled the aftereffects of life on *Eulenspiegel* in a journal entry:

I awoke at Julie's house but believe I am still on the Eulenspiegel. *The lights that cast shadows on the wall move, and in doing so, enforce the illusion I am spinning, almost helplessly on the raft. I cannot reconcile the difference between the interior of her room and the interior of the shack onboard the raft. Sitting up in bed, I feel as though I am in two distinct places at once. Neither reality really works and so the two remain blended and I am totally confused. I get up and notice the street IS the river and the river IS the street. This is no dream. I am fully awake.... I realize ... and I must actually tell myself ... I have taken a "place" from St. Louis to Denver and am now in Julie's house in Boulder.... I returned to bed thinking that I had to check the anchor before retiring.*

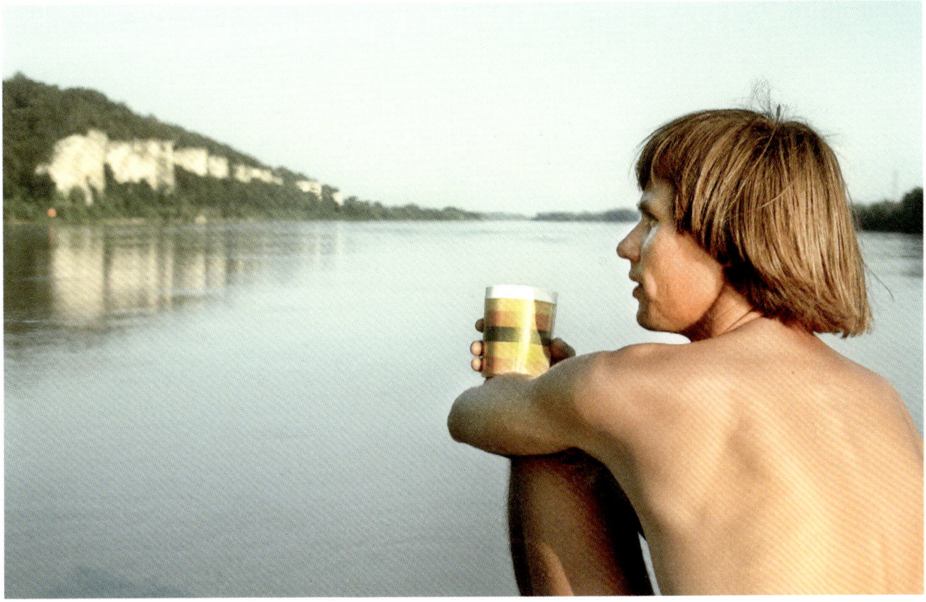

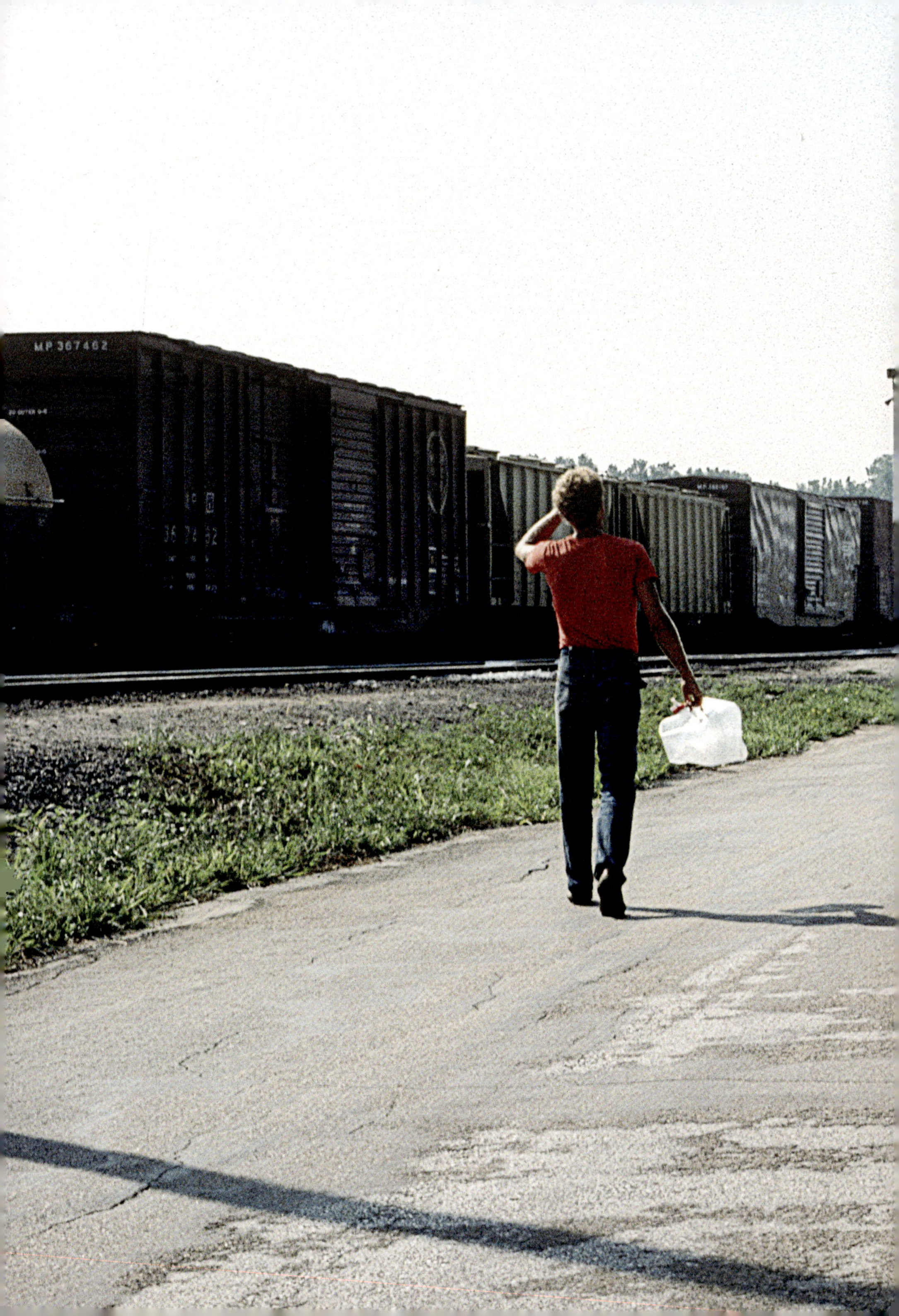
MP 367462

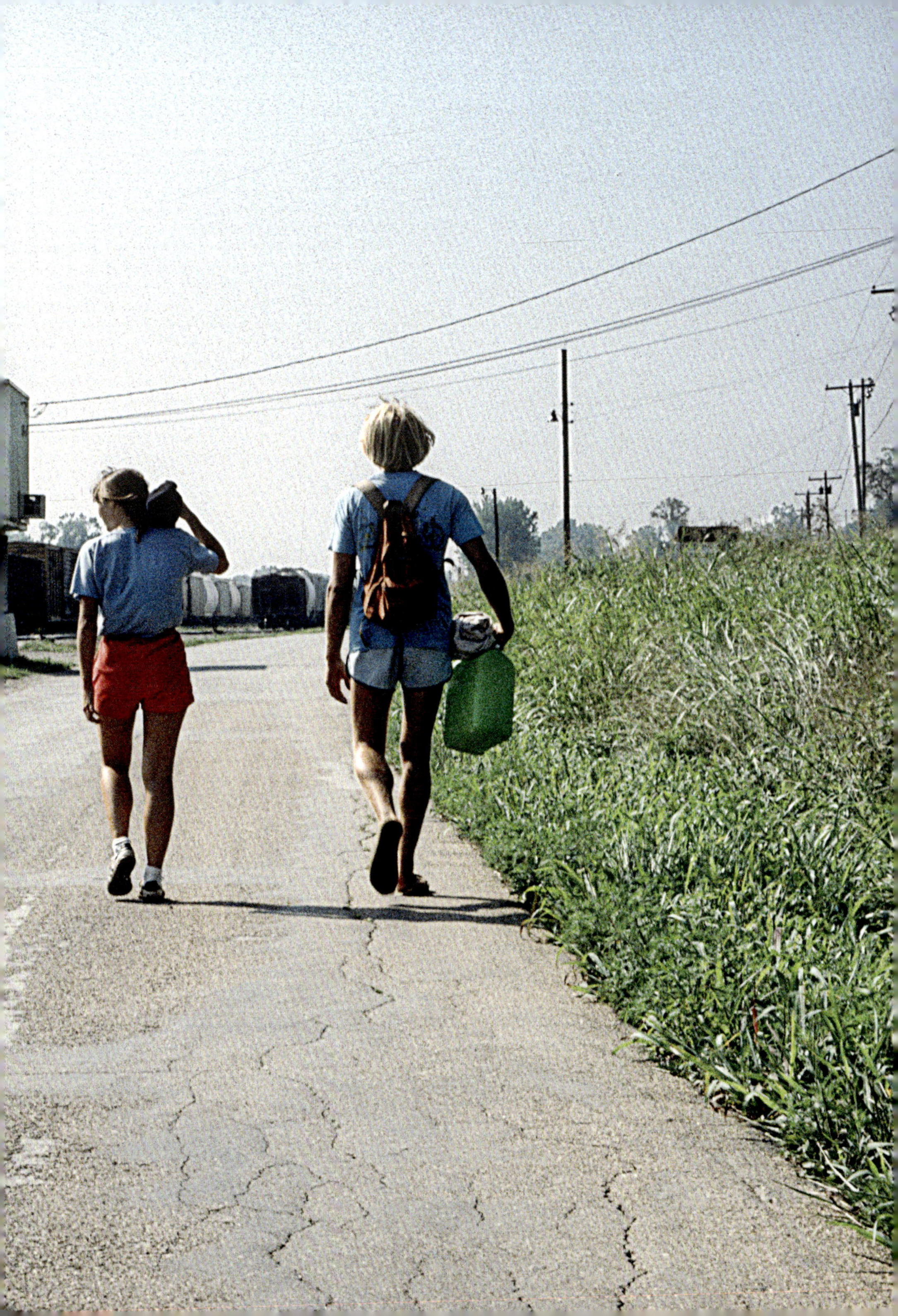

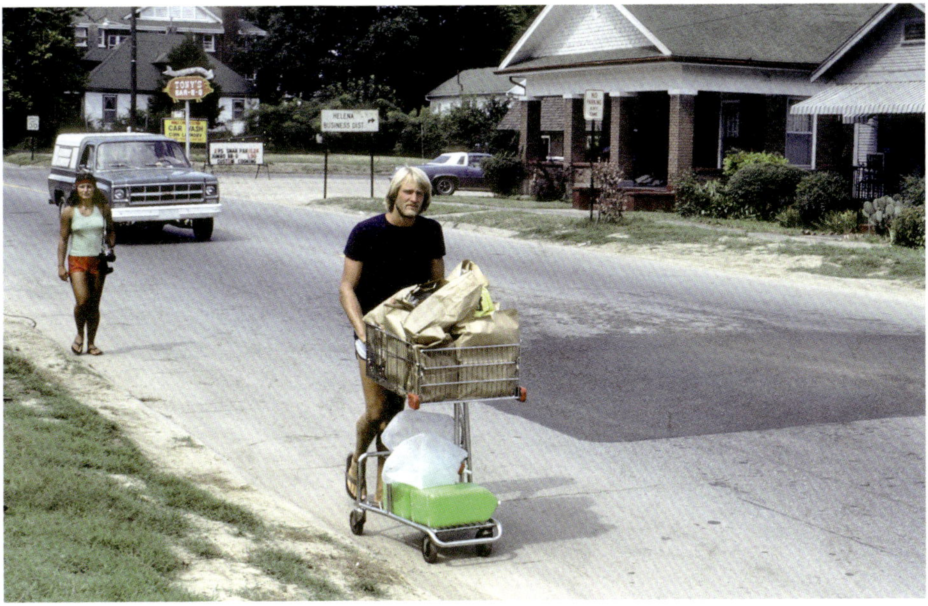
TONY'S
BAR-B-Q
CAR WASH
HELENA
BUSINESS DIST.

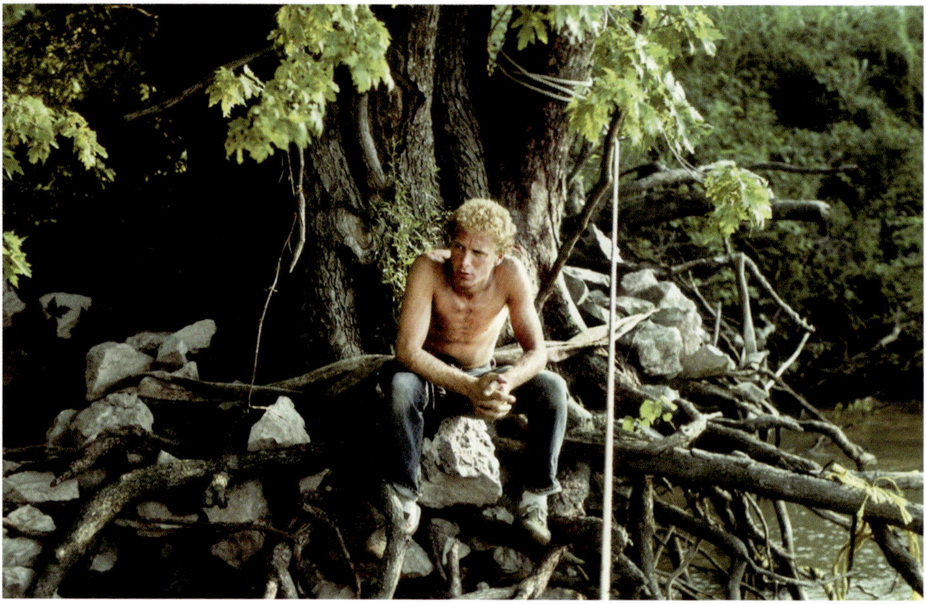

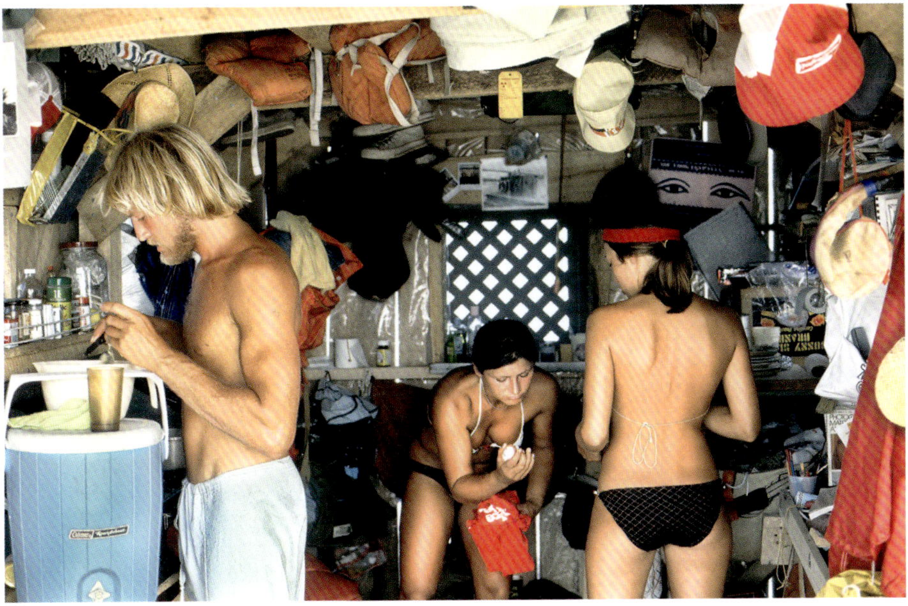

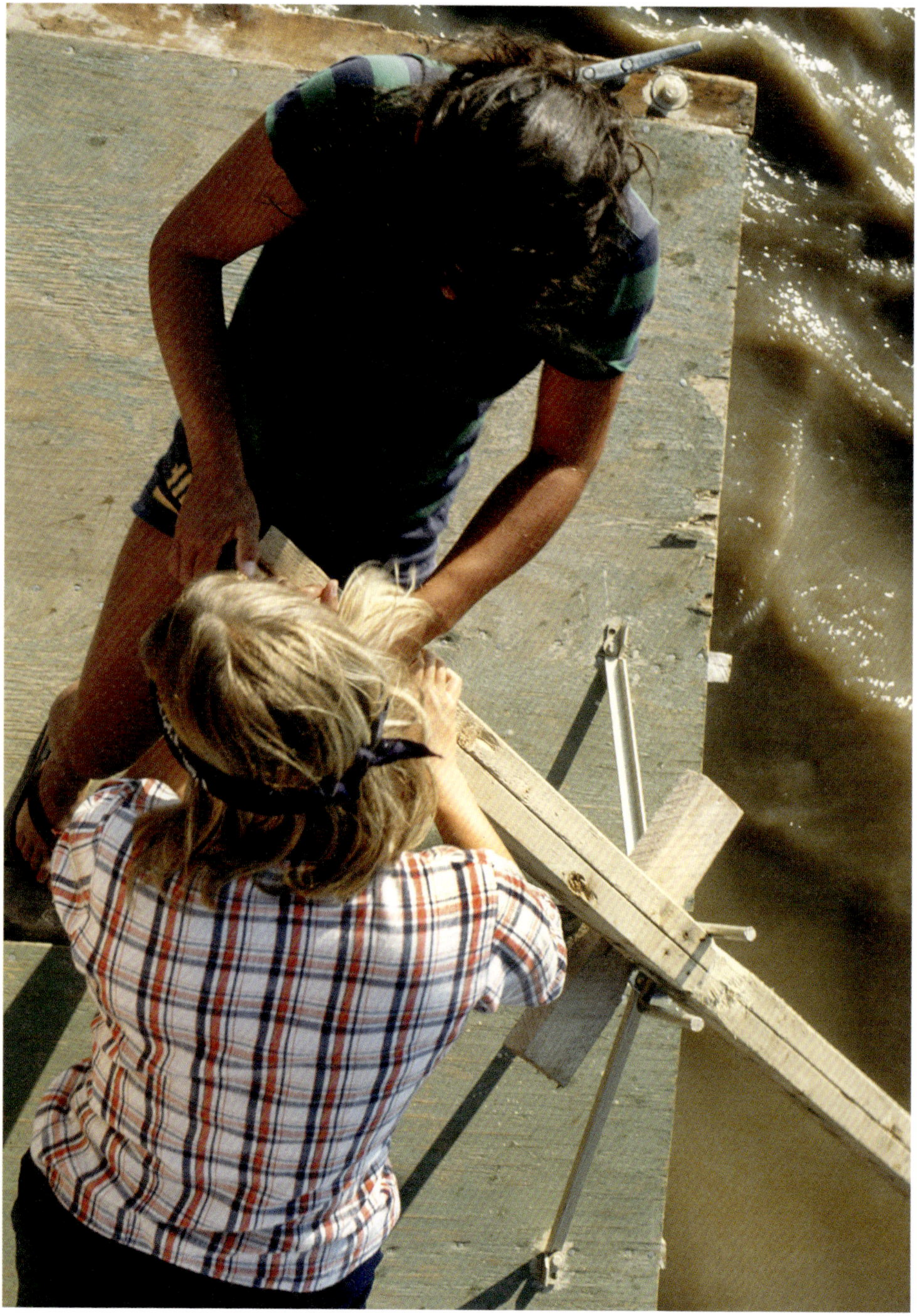

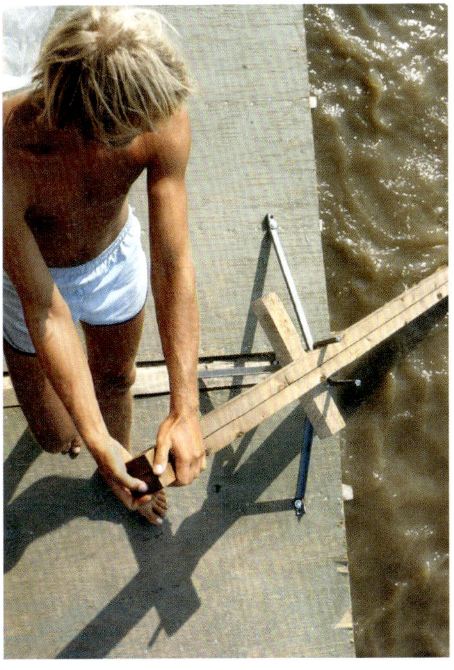

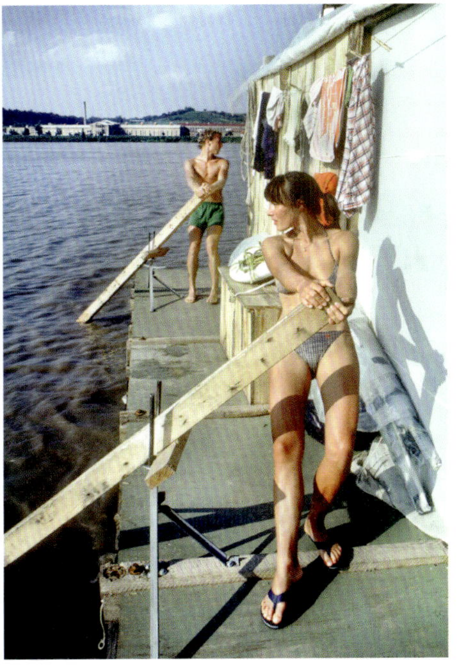

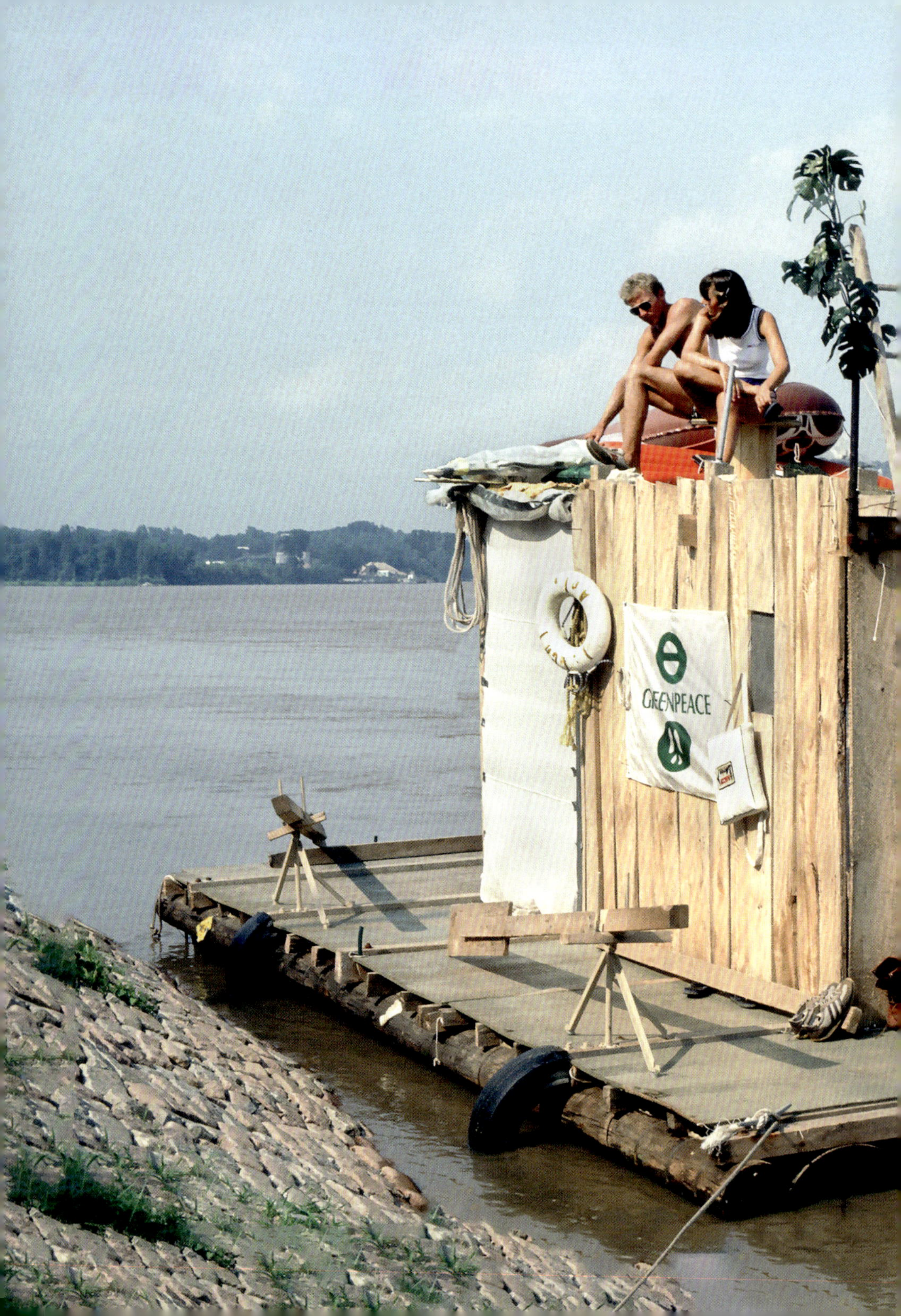
GREENPEACE

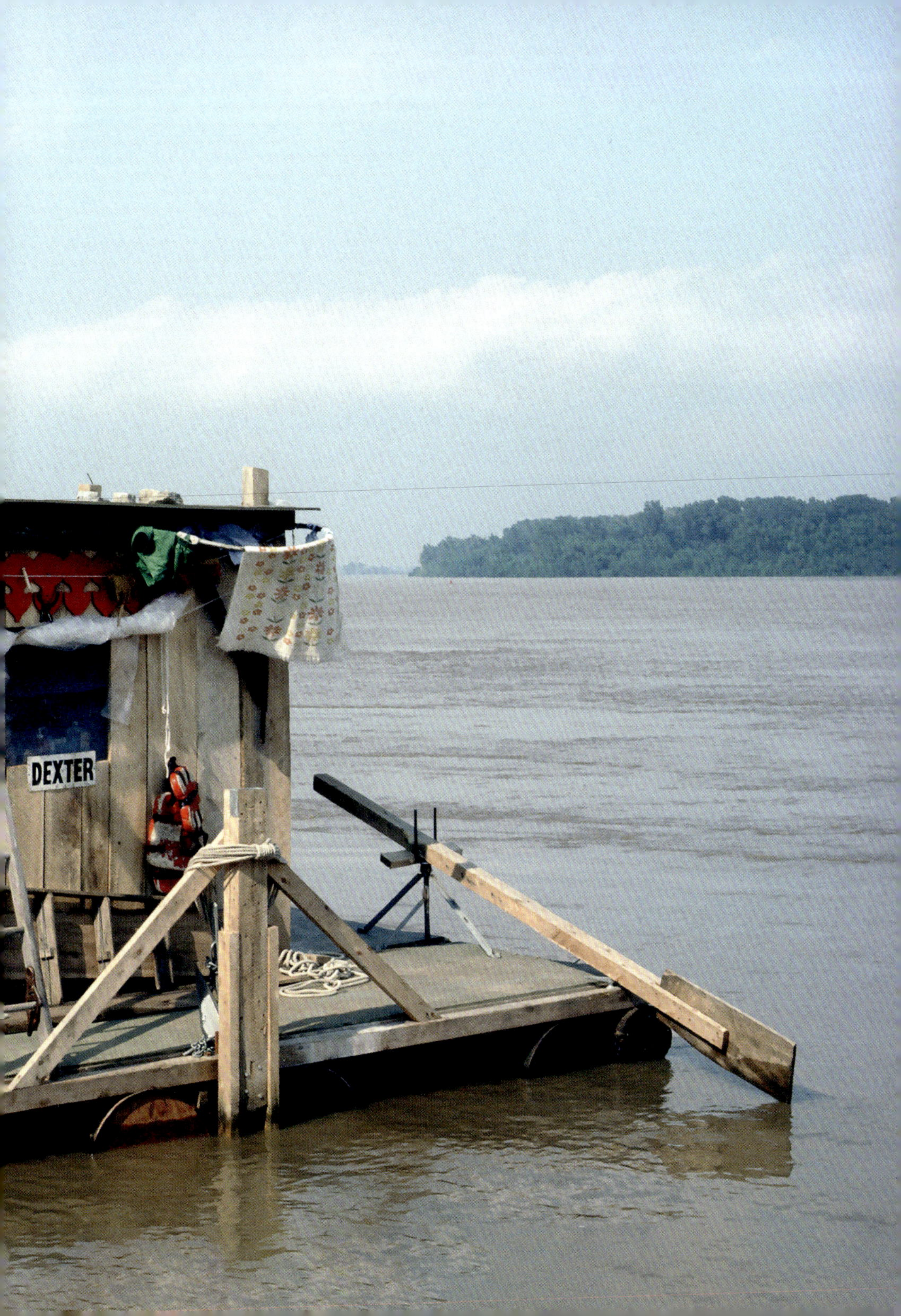
DEXTER

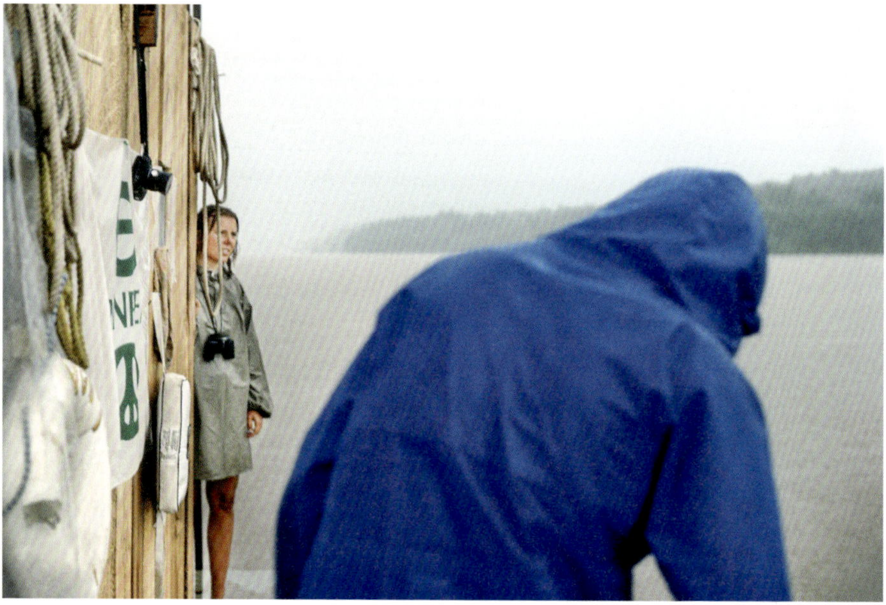

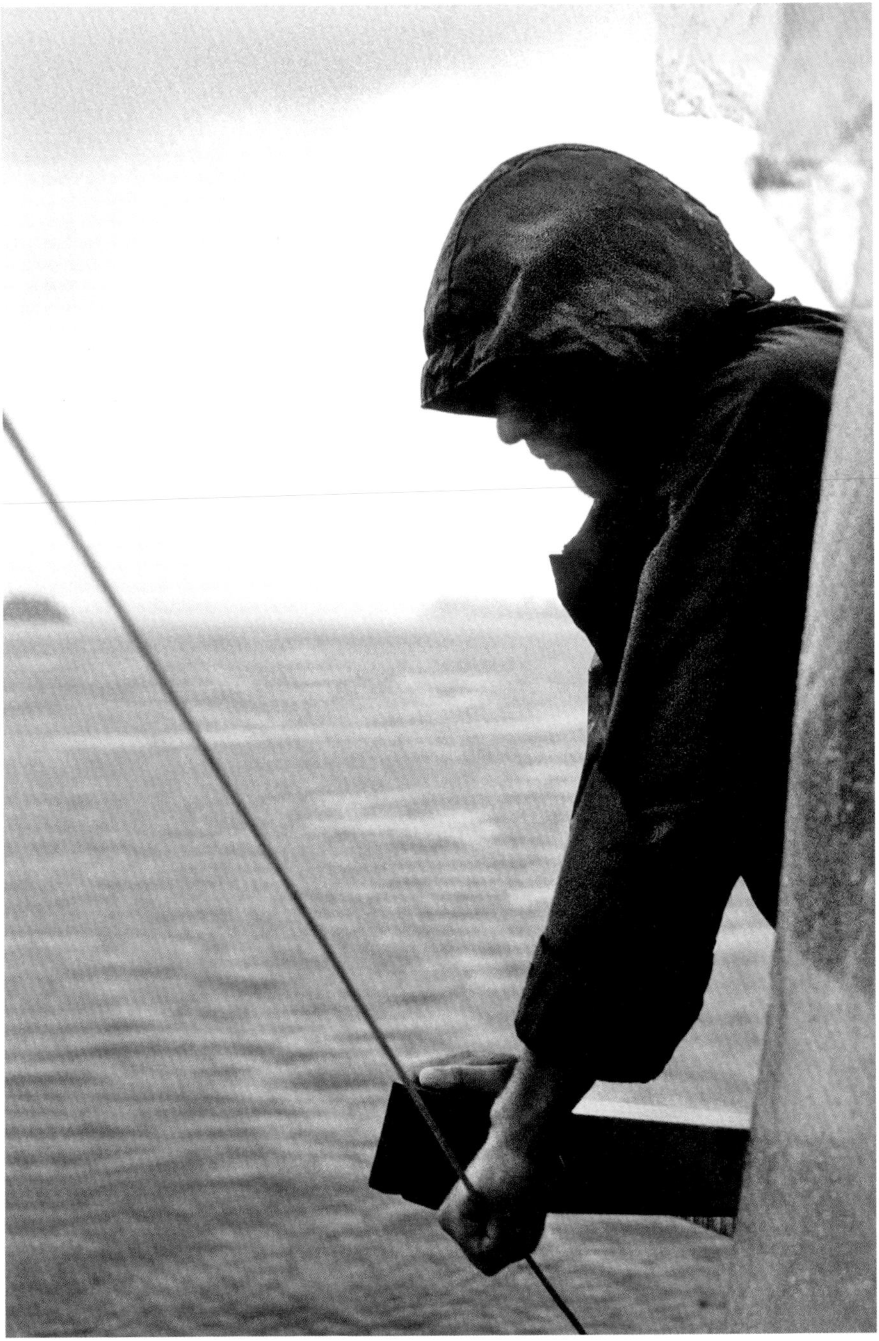

A "chute" or "cutoff" is a shortcut for water flow across a meander in a river created by erosion. It's like a path between the two sides of a road's hairpin turn. The chute is either a creek or a dry wash during low water. During high water, like we were experiencing in this portion of the river, the chute fills with water from the main channel. The current running into the upriver end of a chute can be overwhelming, especially for muscle-driven watercraft like ours, acting like a giant vacuum cleaner sucking in the unwary.

Eulenspiegel passed too close to a chute opening south of Memphis and started barreling toward its entrance. We recognized what was happening early enough to toss our anchor overboard as we entered the chute, since we had no idea where it would take us. This bit of quick thinking gave us some time to figure out what to do.

First, we tried pulling the raft up the anchor rope against the strong current in the chute to inch the raft back into the river's main channel. The idea was to pull ourselves up the rope, reset the anchor further away from the chute, and then pull ourselves up again. Rinse, repeat. That did not work. After an extended mulling of our limited and unattractive alternatives, we finally decided to haul in the anchor and take our chances.

To prepare for our journey into an unknown darkness, we made headlights out of two gas lanterns with aluminum-foil reflectors. We mounted them on the forward canopy of the upper deck, and they threw out enough light to kiss the trees on each bank of the chute. We could see that the water was so high that the solid ground on either side of the raft was flooded, with only tree trunks and branches exposed above the water. Creatures of all sorts, including snakes, made for the high ground in these branches. We took our positions at the oars, or "sweeps," maneuvering the raft into the center of the chute so as not to slam into tree branches and knock a menagerie of river critters onto our deck.

It was quiet, except for the crickets and swiveling oar locks, for what seemed an eternity until we heard the faint sound of falling water up ahead. That sound grew louder and louder. "Oh shit, a waterfall!" Tom was on one of the back oars as we approached it. Light from our makeshift headlights caught the whitewater ripples flowing over the dam. Tom watched the head of the crewman on the front sweep drop down about three feet as all thirty-two barrels broke the night silence, rumbling over a stone dam. Warm river water rushed over Tom's bare shins as the bow dipped deep beneath the water. The raft promptly popped up like a cork on the other side of the dam.

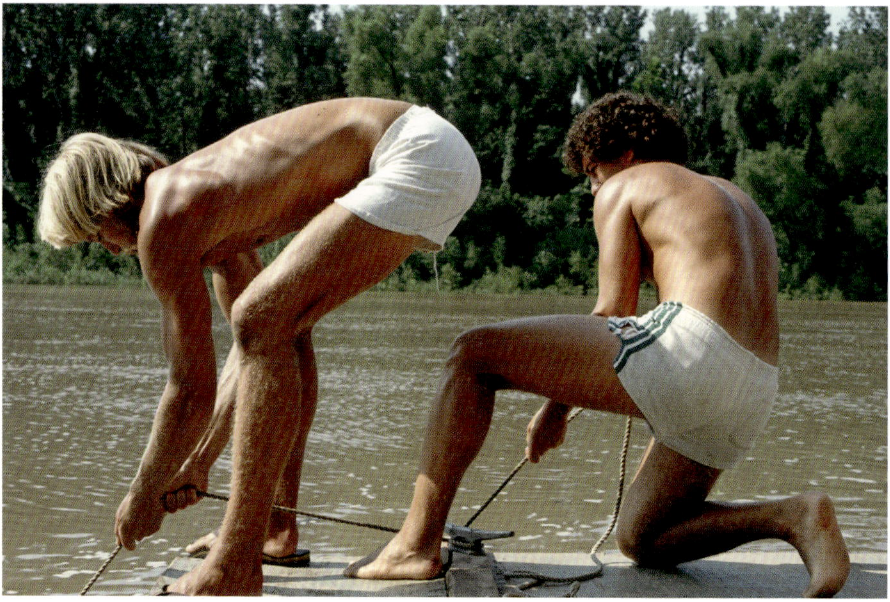

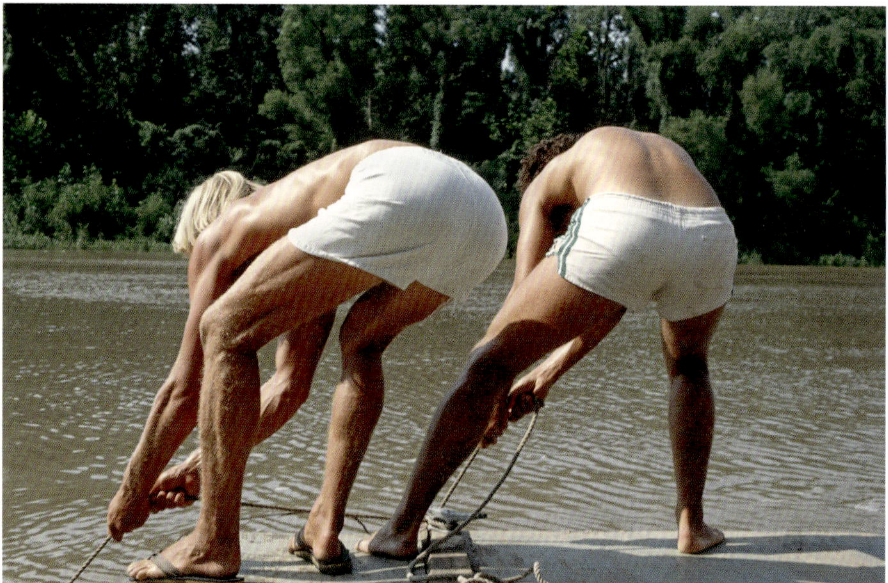

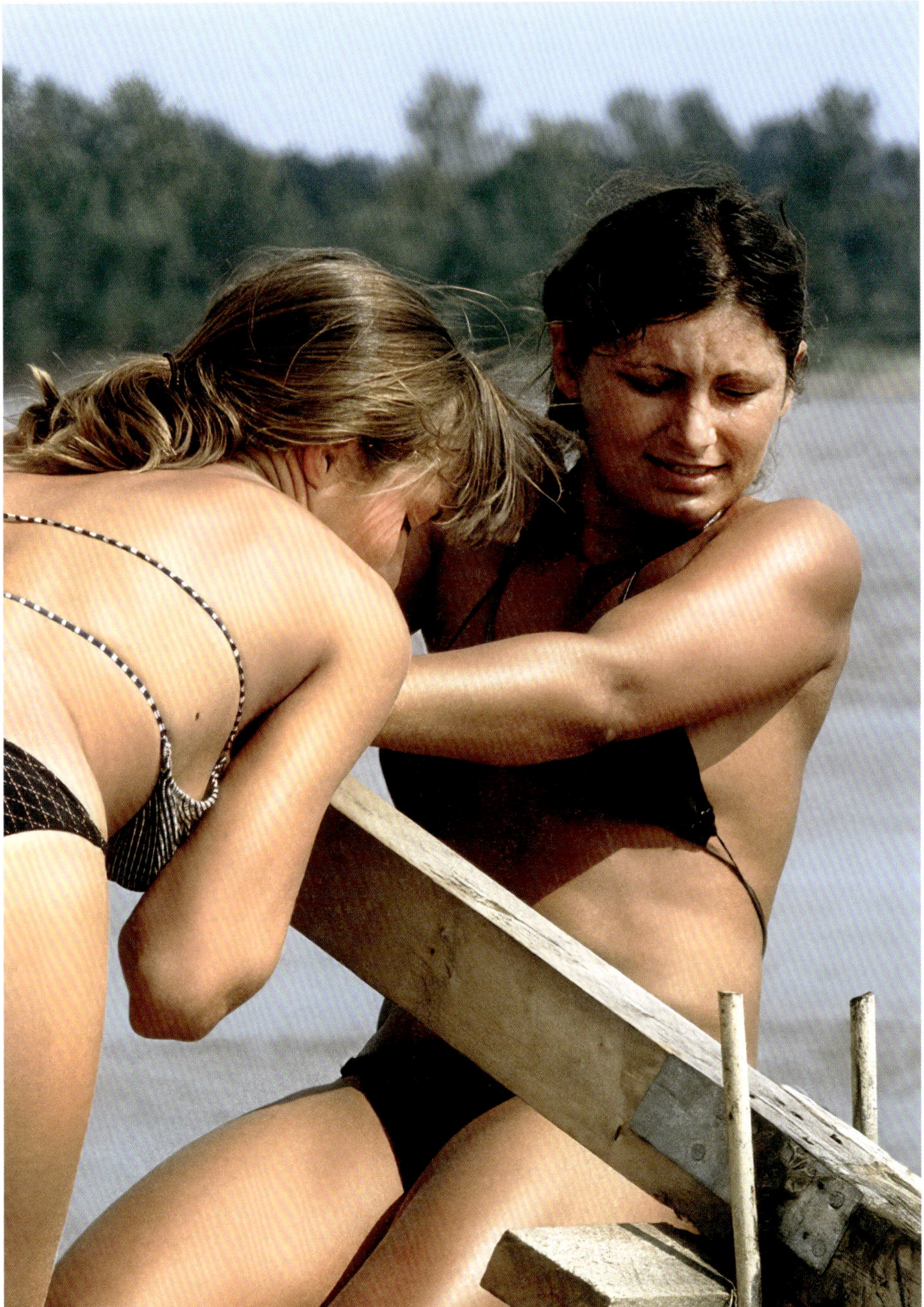

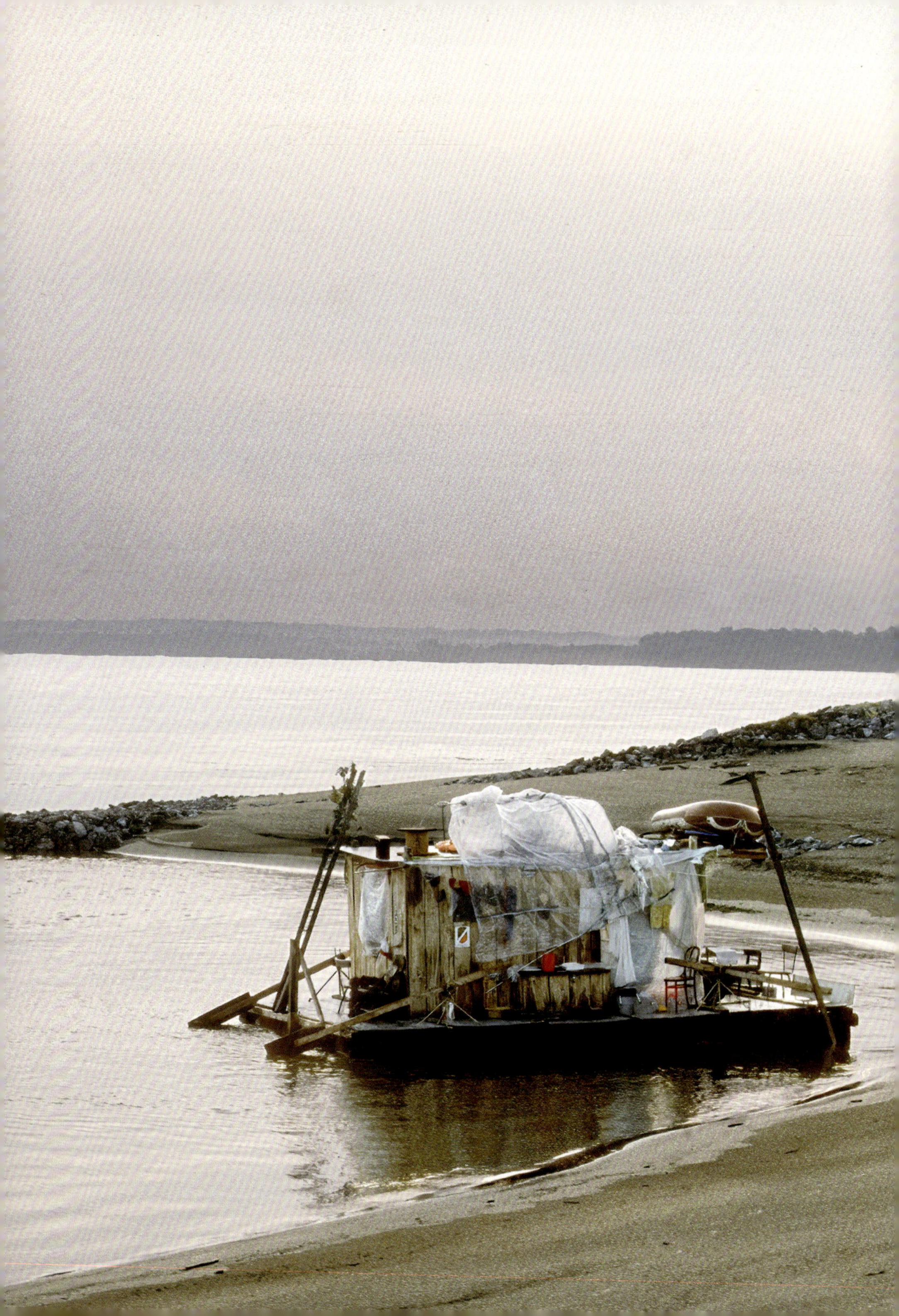

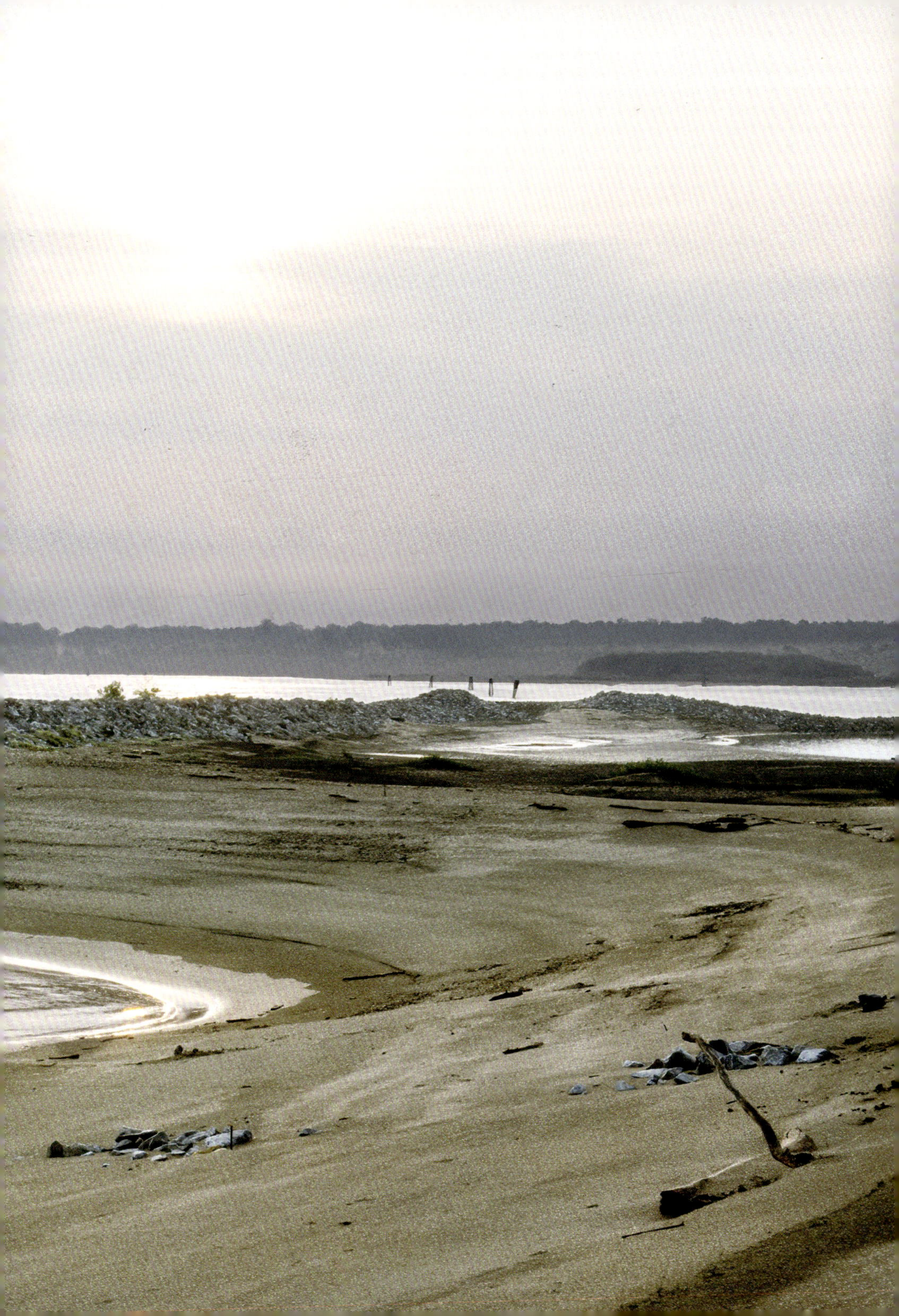

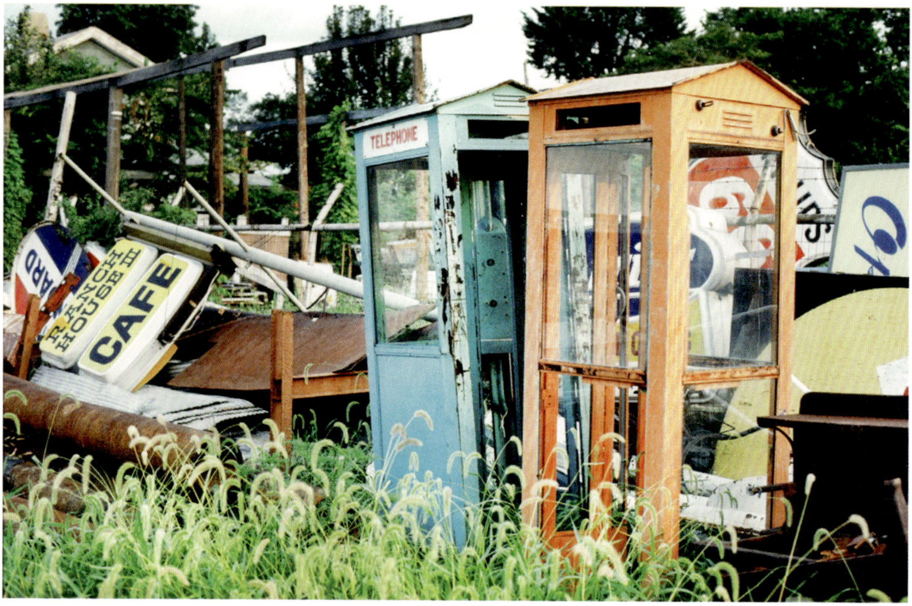
TELEPHONE
CAFE
RANCH HOUSE II

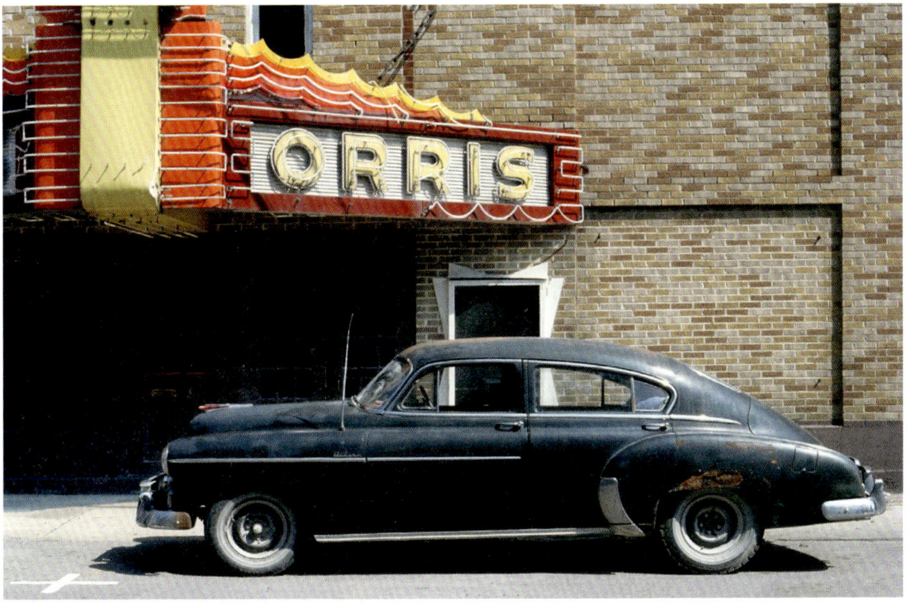
ORRIS

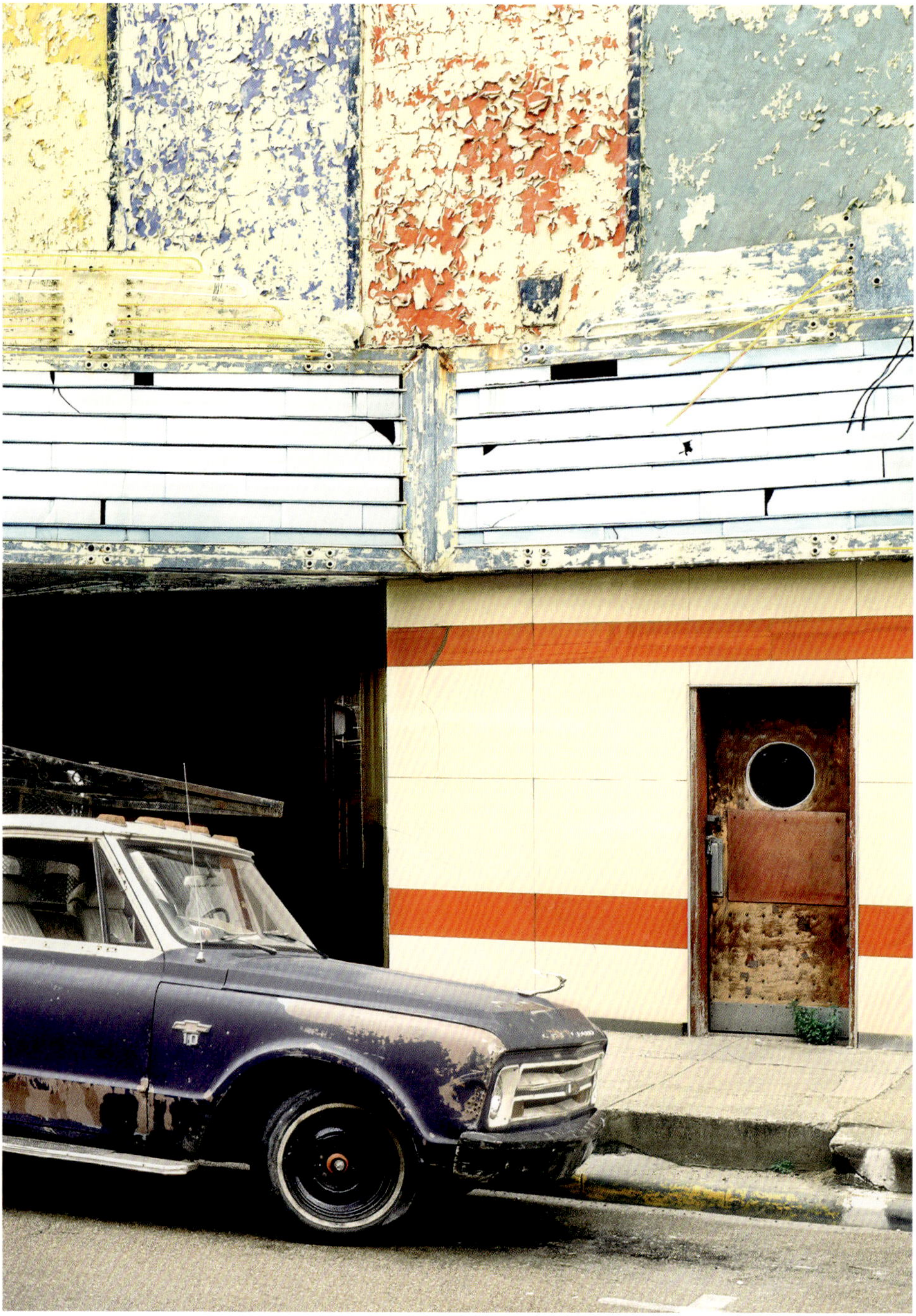

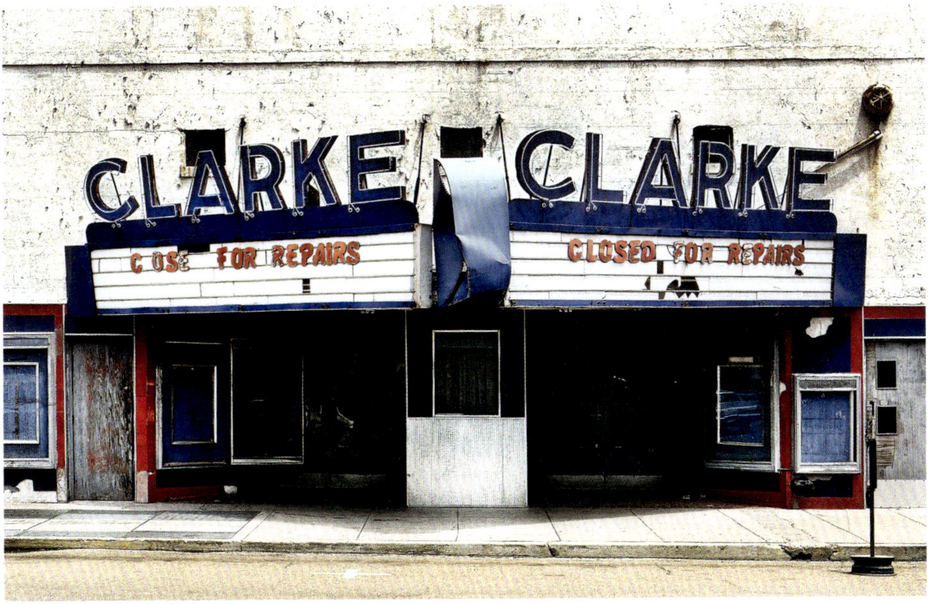
CLARKE
C OSE FOR REPAIRS
CLARKE
CLOSED FOR REPAIRS

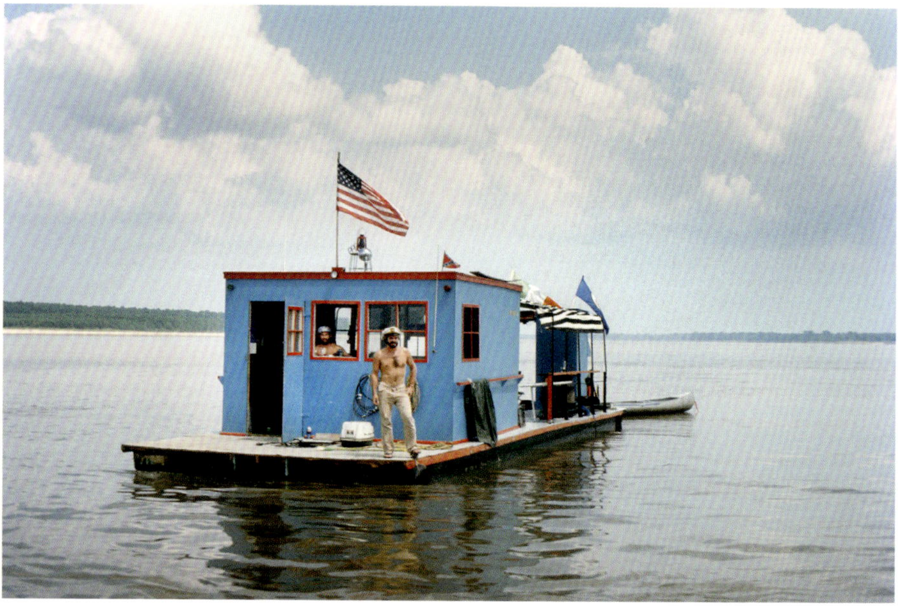

Lance Riley was a seasoned Minneapolis attorney who gave up his practice to build a raft and ride it down the length of the Mississippi River. Lance's raft, which he christened *L'Étoile du Nord*, sported an enclosed cabin and was powered by two used outboard motors. *Eulenspiegel* crossed paths with *L'Étoile du Nord* in Cape Girardeau, Missouri, and we met up again in Memphis, Tennessee, where a good-natured race to Vicksburg, Mississippi, ensued. After beating *Eulenspiegel* to Vicksburg, Lance and his raftmate, Mitch Fruge, traveled along beside us down the Mississippi to Natchez, where we spent a couple of days together before Lance and Mitch headed off down the Red River to look for work on the oil rigs off the coast of Texas, and *Eulenspiegel* continued its journey down the Mississippi River to New Orleans.

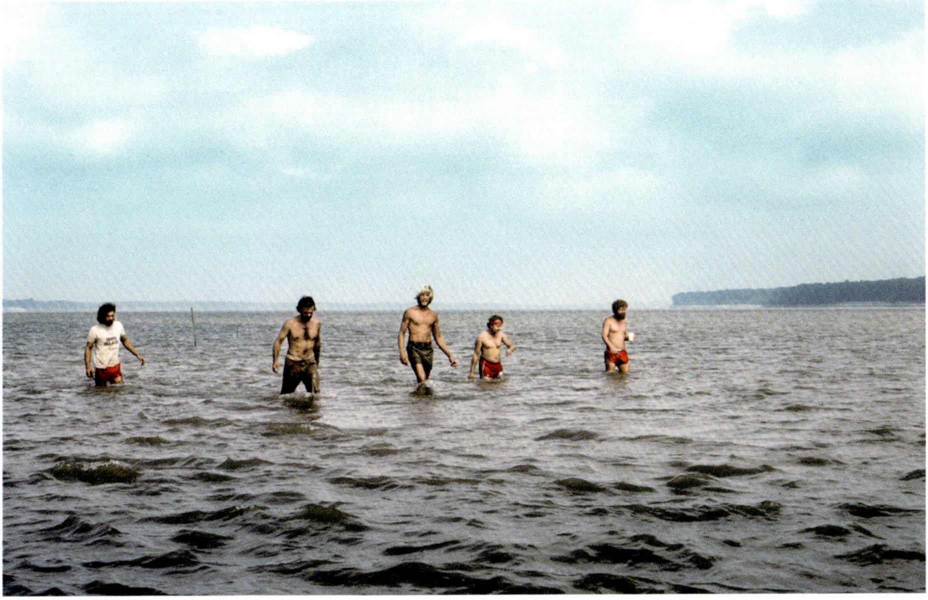

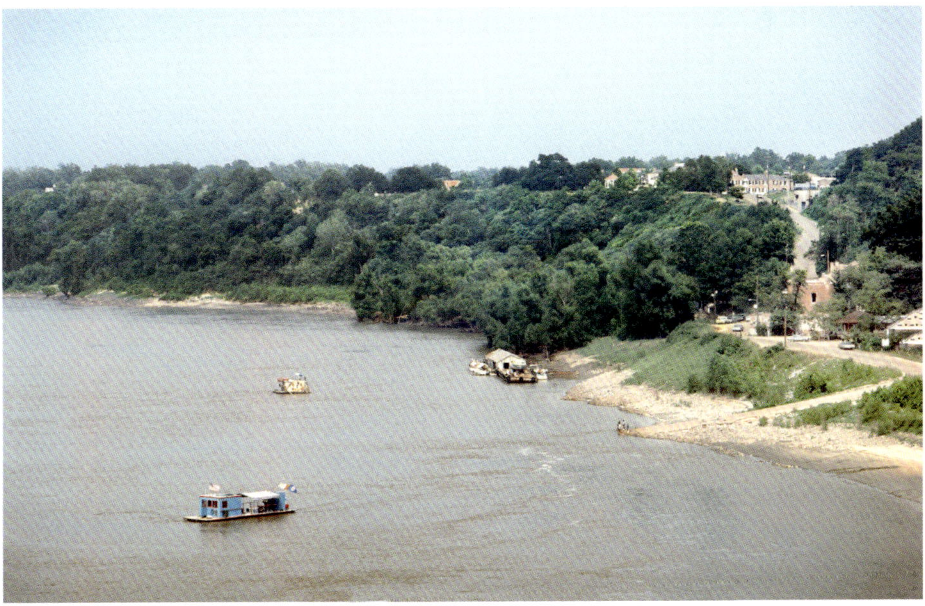

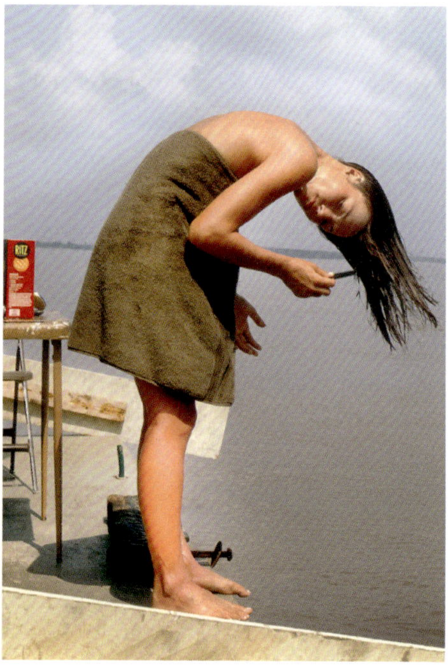
RITZ

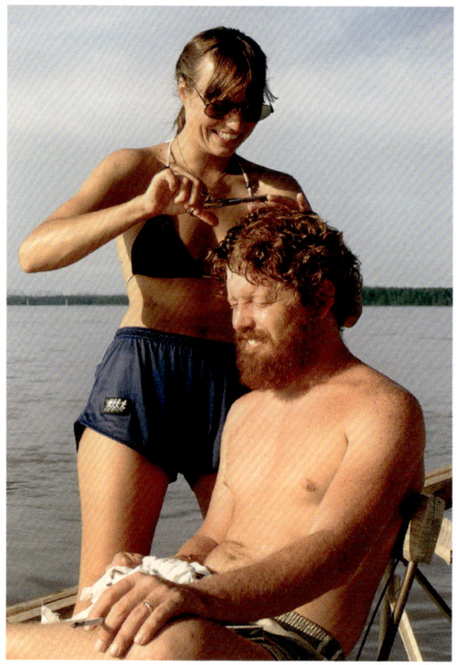

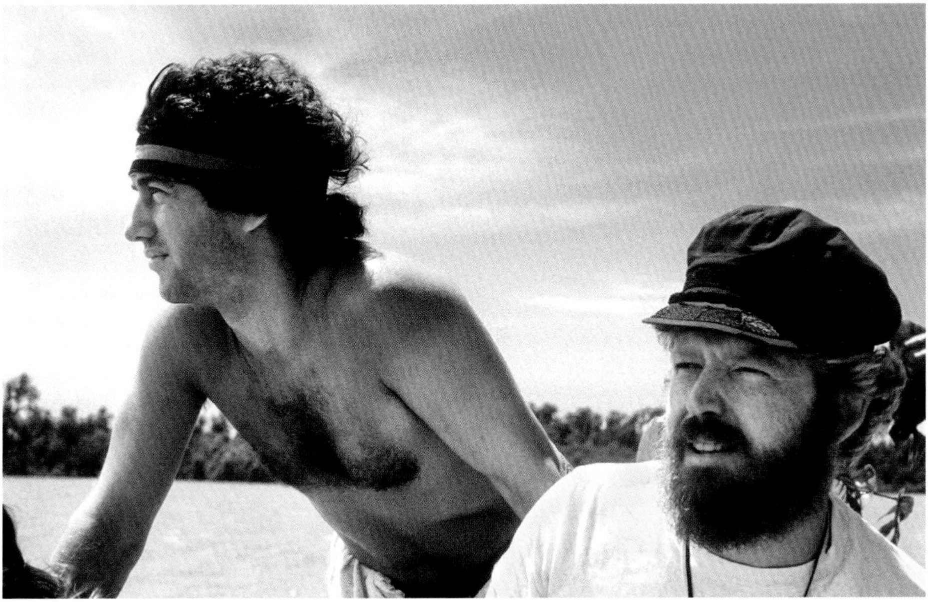

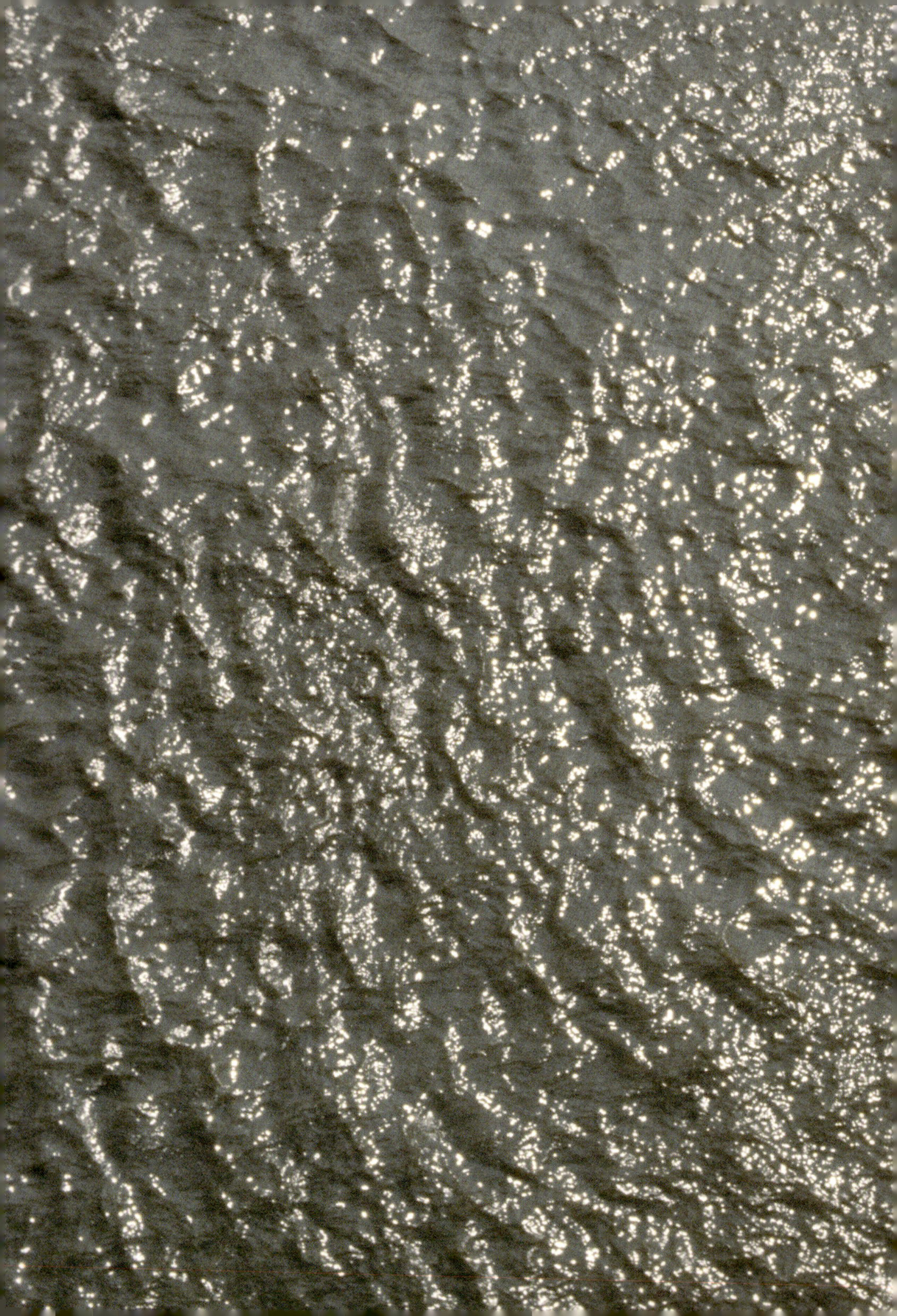

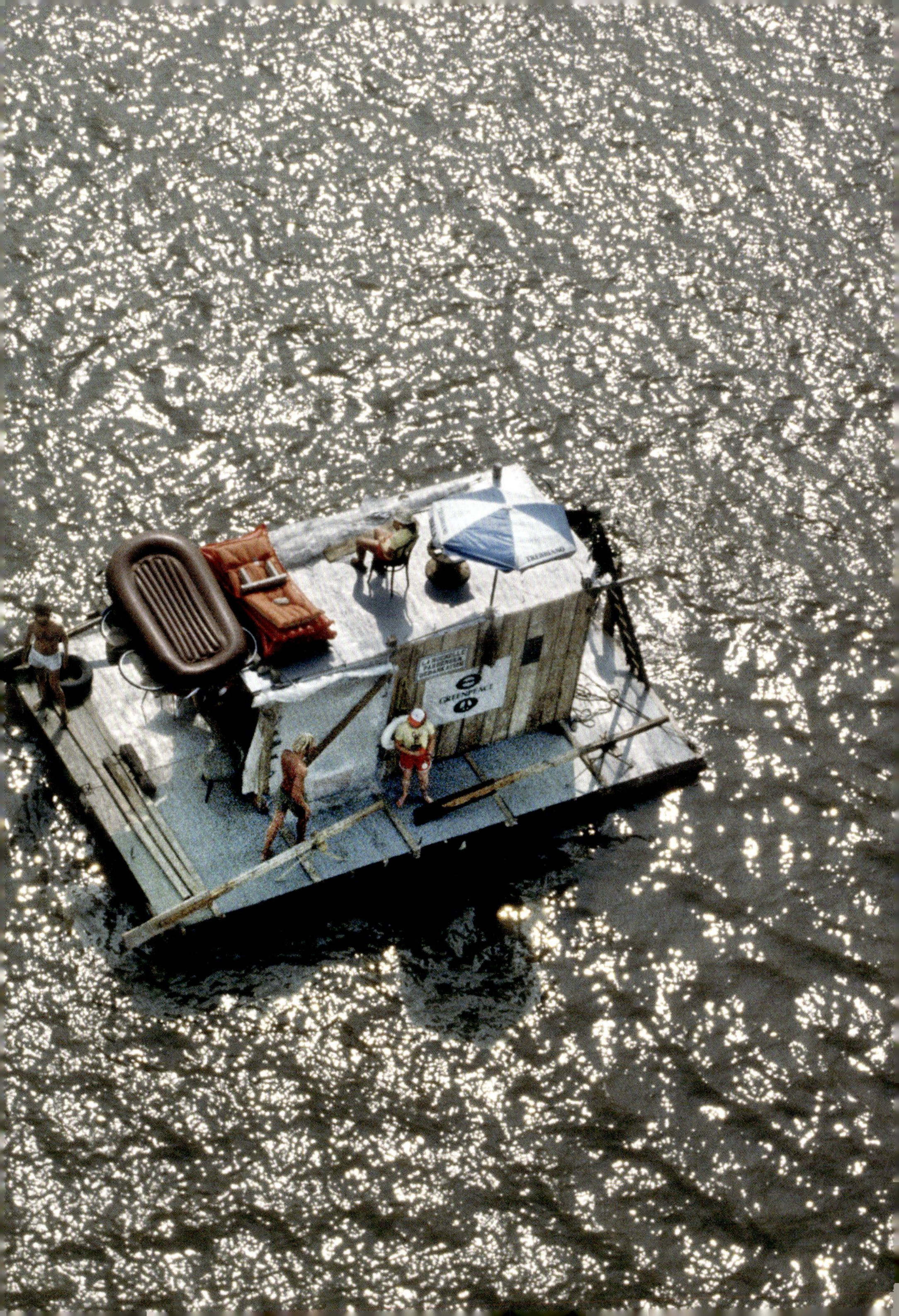

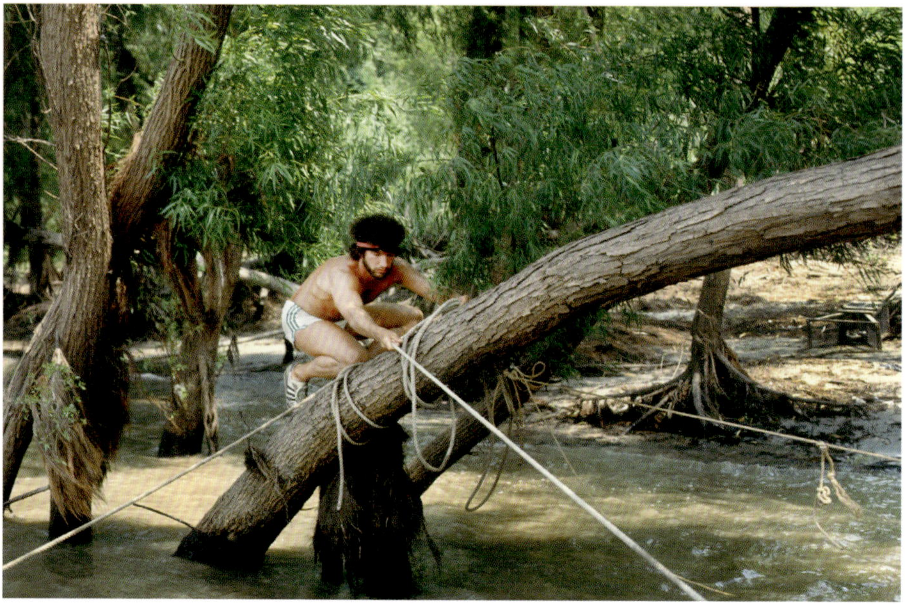

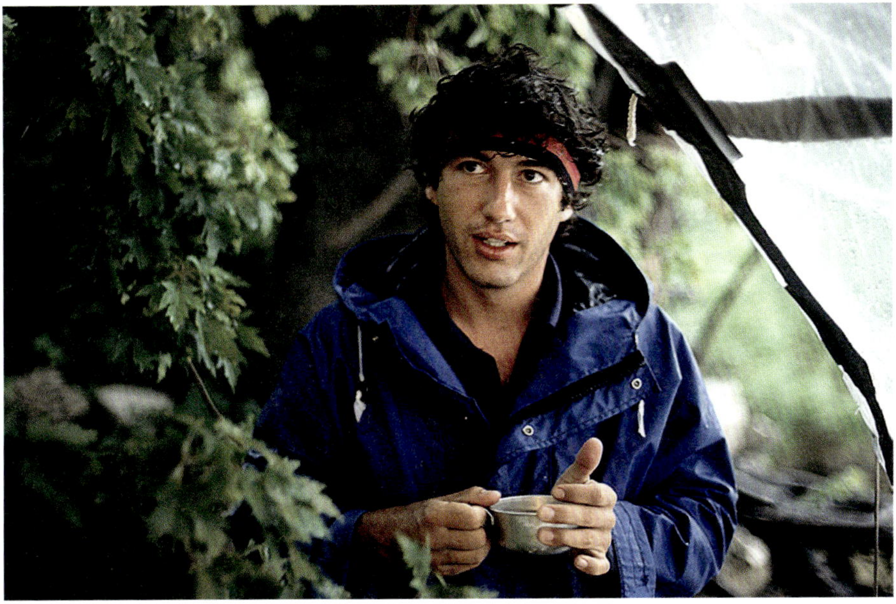

The one bit of truth about this voyage is that I, and the others, I'm sure, will never be the same.

It's going to be a part of us—the river, that is. The river will be a part of us.

Jeff James
September 3, 1981

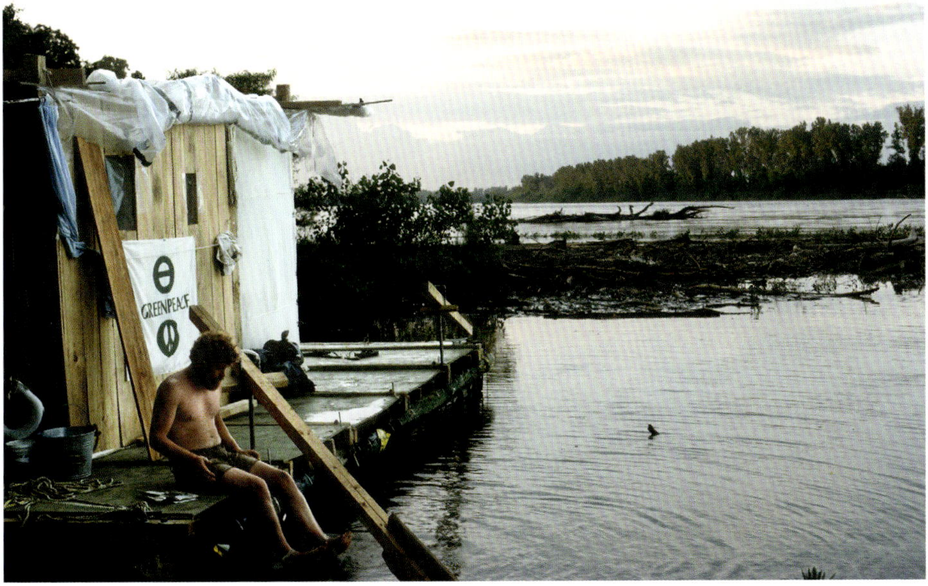

I seemed to have slipped into another world. I remembered the rhythmic sway of the raft, the sound of the river lapping at the bank and the smell of humid fertile soil. Do you remember how dense the fog could become on the river? Sound seemed to hit it and sink. The diffused light from an oncoming barge came upon us before we knew it. Do you remember the hot sun slow simmering us to syrup and how the shade was not much better?... How about the frantic persistence of an alpha fly showing subordinates the finer points of antagonism, or how the hum of mosquitoes going silent meant that they had landed? Do you remember the weight of the oars and the subtle resistance of the water like stirring tea in a cup?

Ed Dilgarde
September 12, 2011

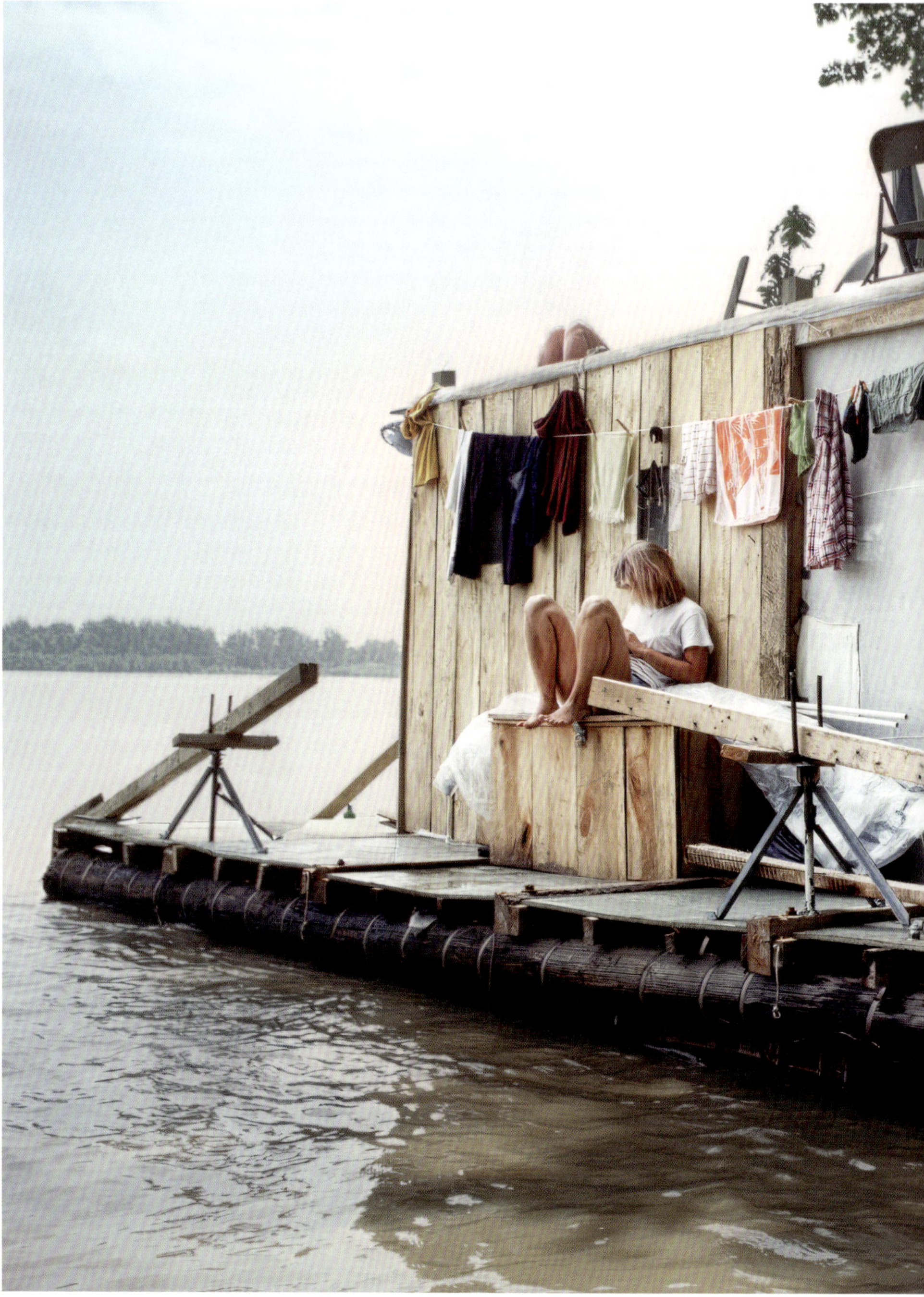

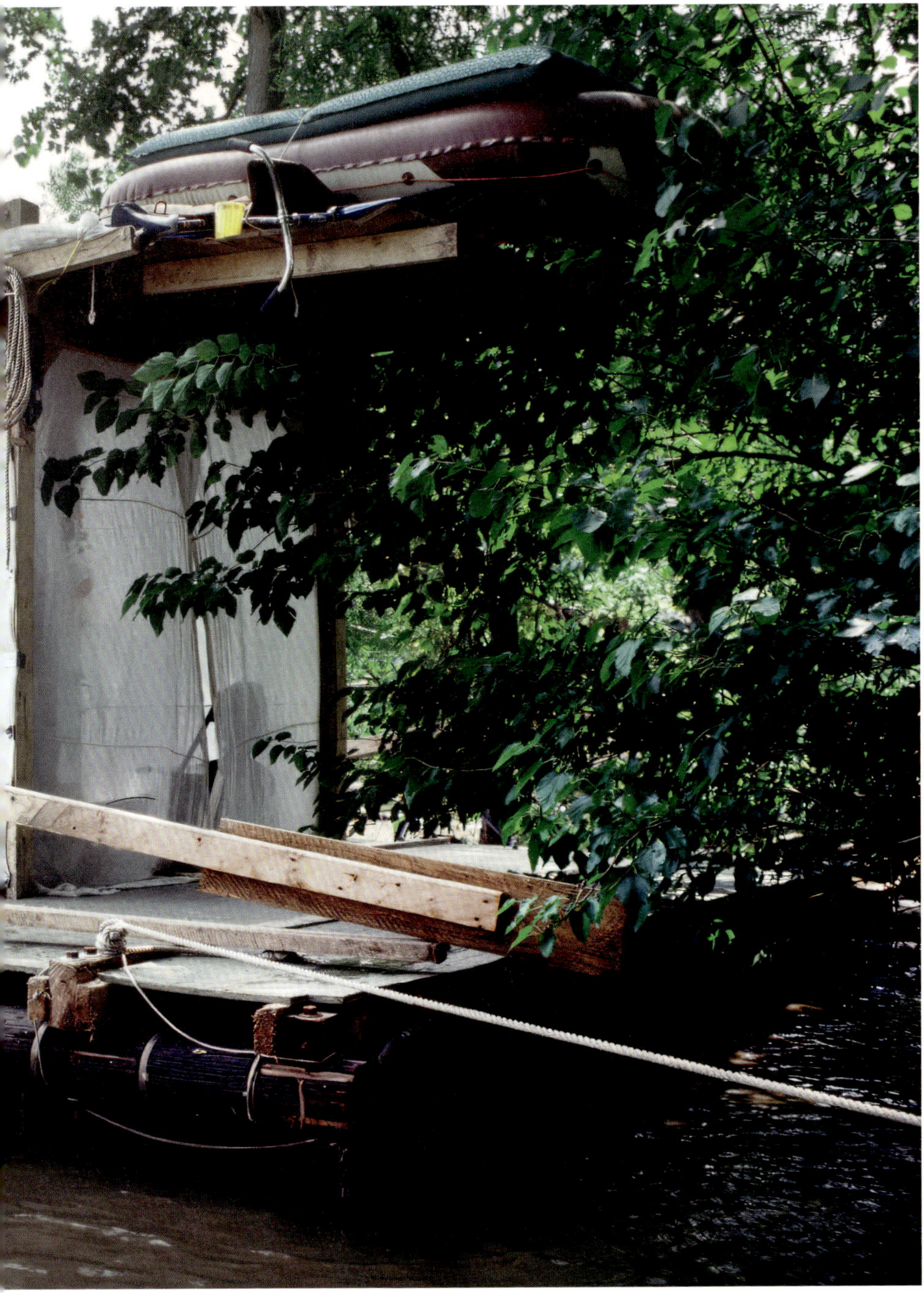

As we approached New Orleans, the river current slowed to a crawl, and we were advancing only a few miles each day (and literally backward one day). So we called on the Harbor Police for the Port of New Orleans for assistance.

A little boat called the *Bali Hai* (Haitian Creole for "paradise-like island") towed us up to Moon Walk Riverfront Park in downtown New Orleans. We anchored in a downpour, got soaked, and felt a collective wave of ambivalence as our trip ended. *Eulenspiegel* had completed its journey slightly over two months after its launch from LaBenite Park. We were then faced with the problem of what to do with the raft, which we had not thought much about in advance.

After a few days, the Harbor Police came back and told us that *Eulenspiegel* was an obstruction to the ocean-going vessels cruising along the river between the Gulf of Mexico and Baton Rouge and had to be moved. After a coordinated sales campaign, the raft eventually sold for forty dollars, barely enough to pay the bus fare home for one crew member.

The buyer was a restaurateur who towed *Eulenspiegel* from the Mississippi River up the Atchafalaya River, where he dropped it off at his eating establishment. He filled the main deck with chairs and tables for guests waiting to be seated in the main dining room. *Eulenspiegel* served the seafood restaurant and its guests for many years until a hurricane severely damaged it in the mid-1980s. The restaurant's owner punctured the raft's oil drums so that it sank slowly to the bottom of the Atchafalaya River.

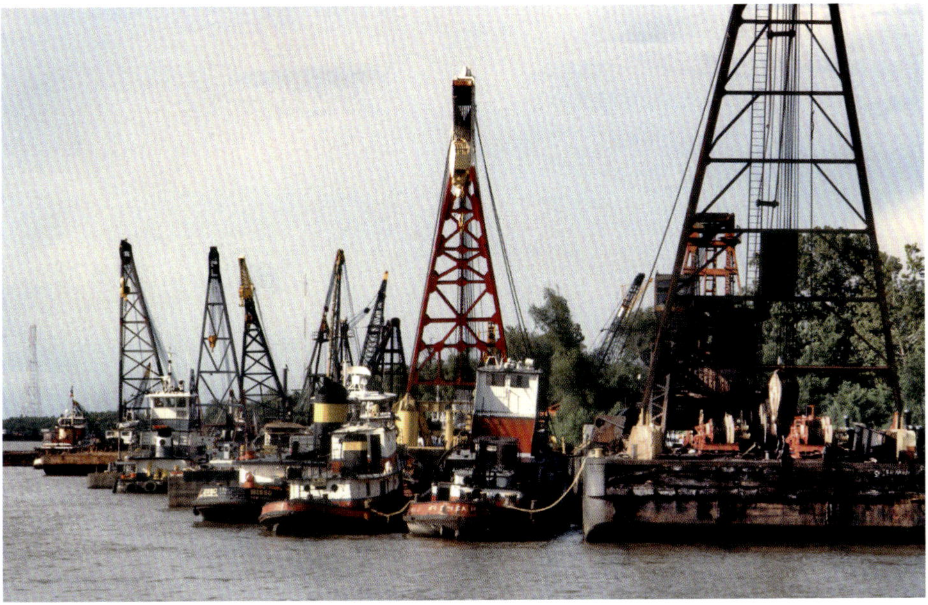

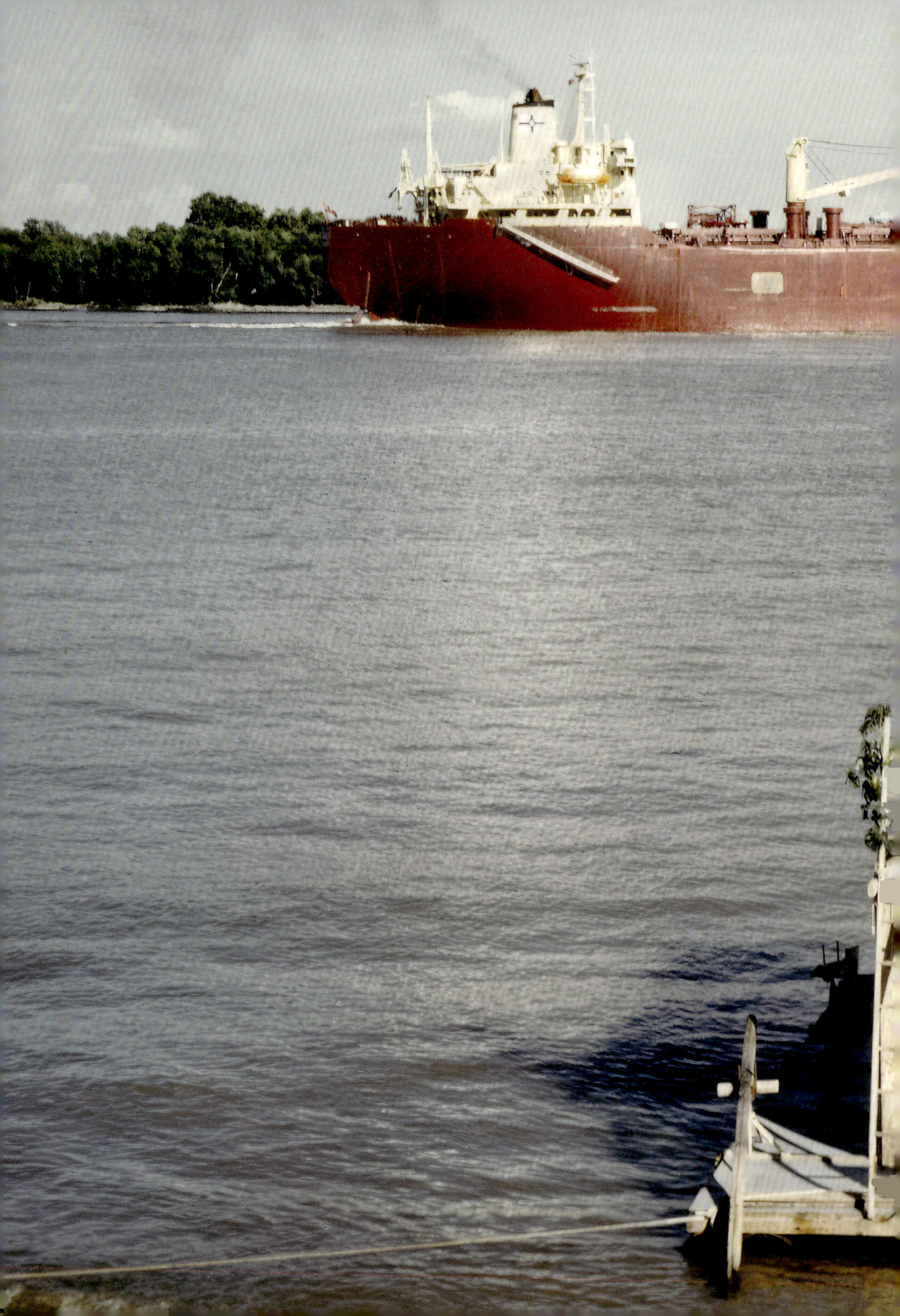

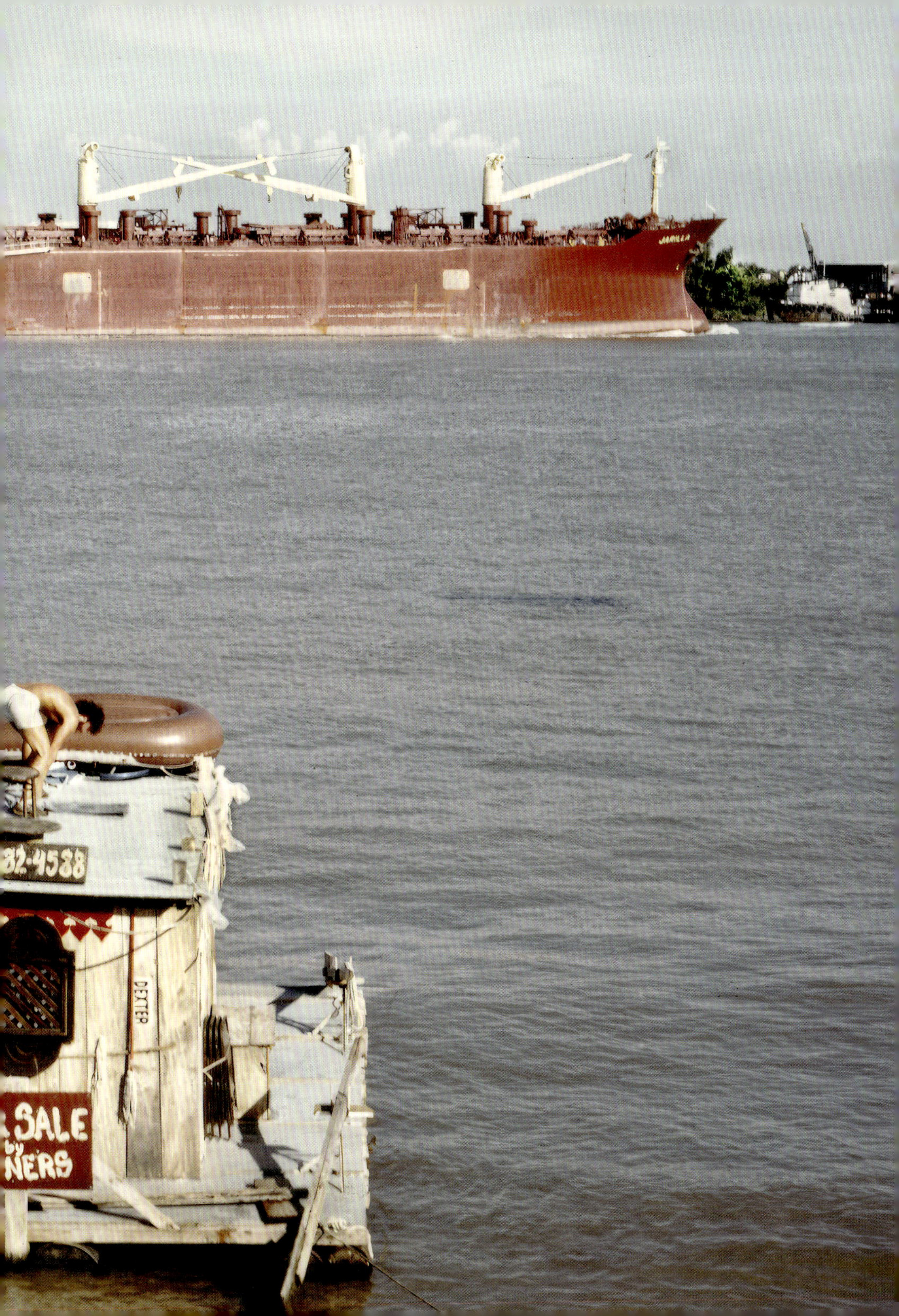
82-4588
DEXTER
SALE
by
NERS

PLATELIST

63 “Something to tell the family about.”

64a “Throttle back.”

64b Tossing a Line

66-67 The mile-wide Mississippi River gave us a new perspective on our place in the world.

69 Cleg and the white limestone cliffs overlooking the Missouri River.

70-71 We spent an awful lot of time fetching potable water while floating down the biggest river in North America.

73 This is Helena, Arkansas. We did not live off the land for the most part, but rather off the local grocery stores. (Photo credit: Eva Ohrner-Bauersachs.)

74 Bill has moored the raft to a tree. (Photo credit: Eva Ohrner-Bauersachs.)

75 Life on *Eulenspiegel.*

76 Linda and Christa double-crew the new, enhanced oar locks we had made for us by a blacksmith in Dexter, Missouri.

77a Bill and Evi test the fortified oar locks. (Photo credit: Kevin Lowder.)

77b Tom gives them a spin as well.

78-79 Cape Girardeau, Missouri.

80 Sometimes it rained long and hard, which created a temporary respite from the mosquitoes.

81 Jeff James, on leave from his job working offshore oil rigs in the Gulf of Mexico, joined the raft crew in Chester, Illinois.

84a-b Tom and Jeff struggle against the current.

85 Evi and Christa double-crew the oar.

86-87 Sunset and then overnight at a sandy riverbank.

88 Cairo, Illinois, where the Ohio River meets the Mississippi.

89 The Orris Theater in St. Genevieve, Missouri.

90 A closed movie theater in Natchez, Mississippi.

91 Just around the corner in Natchez, I found the Clarke Theatre, which had opened in 1949 and closed permanently in 1980.

92 Lance, Mitch, and *L'Étoile du Nord* (a.k.a *I Spy*).

93a Lance and Mitch had gotten their raft stuck on a sandbar, so we were feeling for the surest path back to the channel. (Photo credit: Eva Ohrner-Bauersachs.)

93b Leaving Natchez in Formation

94a-b In a tangible sense, we had become a family.

95 Jeff and Ed, up top, on watch.

96-97 Slower current on the lower Mississippi enabled me to walk down the bank ahead of the raft and climb onto a bridge to shoot a few pictures from above.

98 Tying Up

99 Jeff's Morning Cup

101 Green Peace

101-102 Alone time was a rare commodity on the raft. (Photo credit: Kevin Lowder.)

105 Awaiting the Next Assignment

106-107 For Sale by Owners (Photo credit: Eva Ohrner-Bauersachs.)

ACKNOWLEDGMENTS

I would like to thank Eva Ohrner-Bauersachs, Scott Sharp, Kevin Lowder, Ed Dilgarde's widow, Noelle Dilgarde, and Cleg Holiman's sister, Shauna Holiman, for allowing me to reproduce some of their writings, photographs, and artwork from the raft trip in this book.

Credit is given for their photographs in the platelist, and for other artwork and writings on the page where they appear. Any photographs or writings not expressly credited are the work of the author.

I would also like to thank Tom Bates, Scott Sharp, Eva Ohrner-Bauersachs, Kevin Lowder, Shauna Holiman, and Noelle Dilgard for their help in collecting and organizing the materials for this book.

I would like to thank Tom Bates for assisting me with the narrative portion of this book and for refreshing my inconsistent memory.

Finally, Tom and I would like to thank Tom's brother, Kansas City resident Greg Bates, whose guidance and contacts with local contractors and media outlets made building *Eulenspiegel* and funding our voyage possible.

Addendum

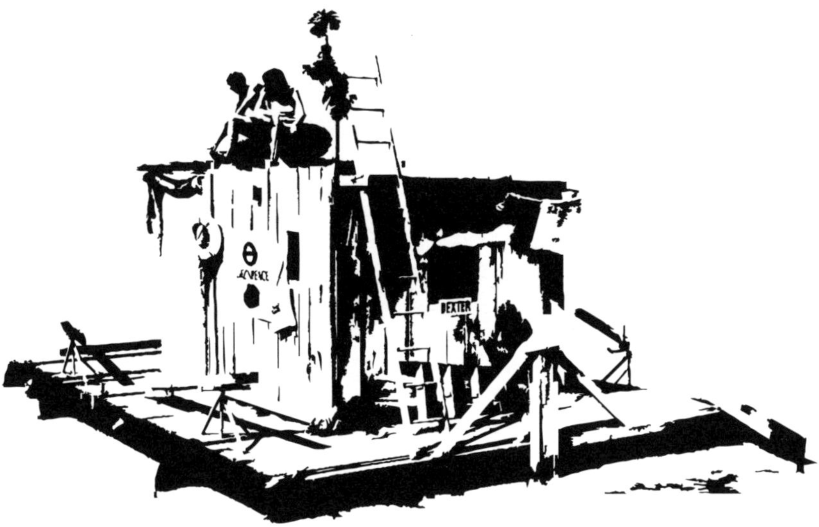

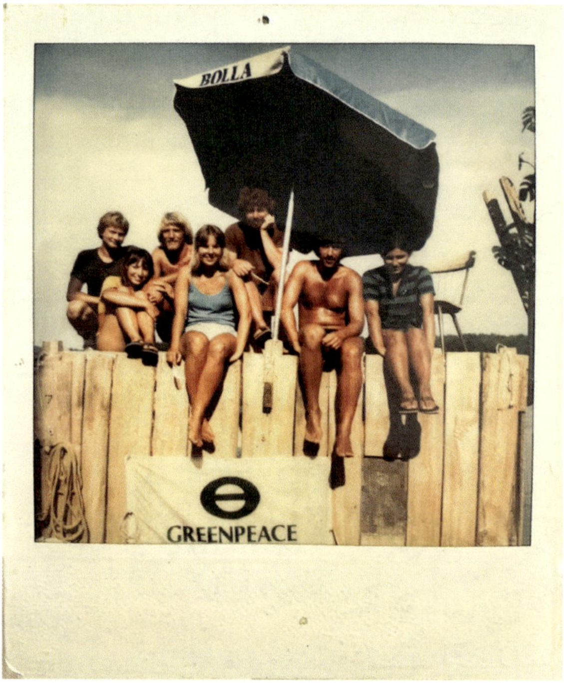

An admirer used their Polaroid camera to take this photograph of the crew and then gave the picture to Ed.

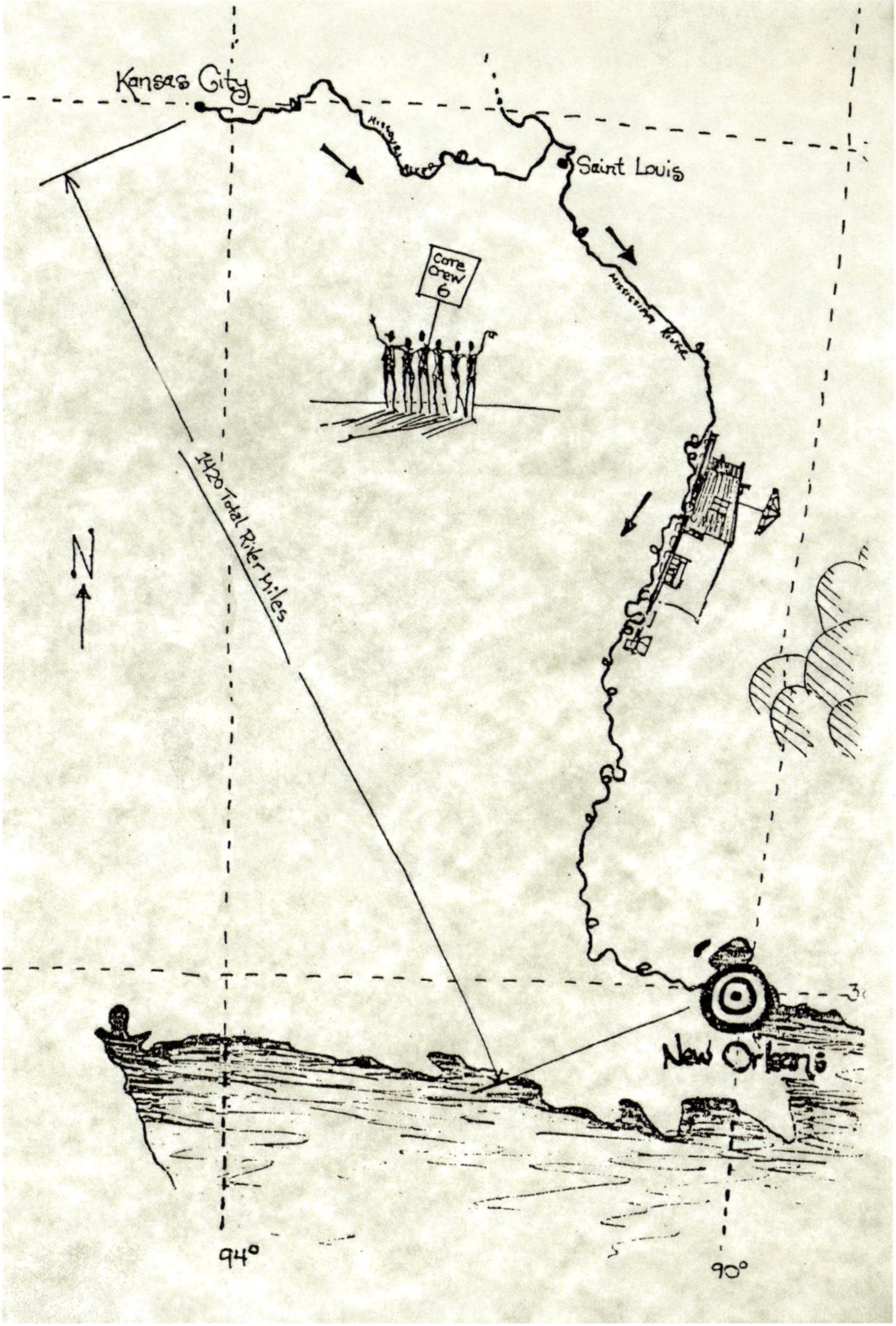

Ed drew this map of the raft's planned path from Kansas City to New Orleans in anticipation of our journey.

ED'S VOYAGE LOG

This is Ed's daily log of *Eulenspiegel*'s progress down the Missouri and Mississippi Rivers from Kansas City to New Orleans.

DATE	STOPS	END MILE	MILES TRAVELLED	BEGINNING TIME	STOP TIME	END TIME	TOTAL TIME
JULY 3	LA BENITE RIVER FRONT PARK (352.7)	327.3	25.4	11:50	–	7:55	8:05
4	LEXINGTON, MO (316.5)	316.5	10.8	12:10	–	3:30	3:20
5		275.1	41.4	7:25	–	9:15	13:50
6	GLASGOW, MO (225.8)	225.8	49.3	7:03	–	10:05	13:02
7		209.3	16.5	3:14	–	8:17	5:03
8	LUPUS, MO (174.6)	174.6	34.7	7:20	4:05	9:08	9:43
9	JEFFERSON CITY, MO (143.8)	143.8	30:8	9:41	–	5:21	7:40
10	HERMANN, MO (97.9)	97.9	45.9	9:00	–	9:20	12:20
11	HERMANN, MO	–	–	–	–	–	–
12	WASHINGTON, MO (68.5)	68.5	29.4	12:30	–	8:40	8:10
13	ST. CHARLES, MO (27.8)	27.8	40.7	11:25	–	9:40	10:05
14		3.4	24.4	11:30	1:57	8:06	6:39
15	ST. LOUIS, MO (179.8)	179.8	17.7	6:43	5:00	10:45	11:02
16	ST. LOUIS	–	–	–	–	–	–
17	ST. LOUIS	–	–	–	–	–	–
18	ST. LOUIS	–	–	–	–	–	–

DATE	STOPS	END MILE	MILES TRAVELLED	BEGINNING TIME	STOP TIME	END TIME	TOTAL TIME
19	ST. LOUIS	–	–	–	–	–	–
20		176.1	3.7	8:00	–	9:30	1:30
21	CRYSTAL CITY, FESTUS, MO (149.6)	130.5	45.6	8:00	2:10	8:52	10:42
22	ST. GENEVIEVE, MO (125.3) CHESTER, IL (110.)	110.0	20.5	7:46	3:50	5:55	6:19
23	(109.8) (106.)	94.1	15.9	12:50	2:00?	8:11	5:21
24	PICAYUNE CHUTE (60.7-54.8)	55.0	39.1	7:20	–	10:30	15:15
25	CAPE GIRARDEAU (52)	52.0	3.0	?	–	?	?
26	CAPE GIRARDEAU, MO	–	–	–	–	–	–
27		41.3	10.7	5:45	–	8:40	2:55
28	CAIRO, IL (5.8)	5.8	35.5	9:10	–	5:32	8:22
29		926.8	23.0	11:45	–	8:15	8:30
30	NEW MADRID, MO (888.5)	888.5	38.3	7:30	–	6:55	11:25
31	CARUTHERSVILLE, MO (846.2)	846.2	42.3	8:26	–	8:15	11:49
AUG. 1	[TENN.]	801.0	45.2	8:20	–	8:45	12:25
2	[TENN.]	764.0	37.0	7:30	–	7:46	12:16
3	MEMPHIS, TN. (735.0)	735.	29.0	9:00	–	5:30	8:30
4	MEMPHIS	–	–	–	–	–	–
5	MEMPHIS	–	–	–	–	–	–

DATE	STOPS	END MILE	MILES TRAVELLED	BEGINNING TIME	STOP TIME	END TIME	TOTAL TIME
T 6		710.0	25	12:15	–	8:10	7:55
F 7	[ARK.]	675.5	34.5	9:15	–	7:50	9:35
S 8	HELENA, AR (663.5)	646.5	29.	7:30	3:30	8:00	9:00
S 9	[ARK.]	598.2	48.3	6:00	–	8:20	14:20
M 10	[MISS.]	555.2	43.0	6:10	–	7:20	13:10
T 11		501.0	54.2	6:17	–	8:20	14:03
W 12	LAKE PROVIDENCE, (483.2)	469.0	32.0	6:45	3:30	8:15	10:00
T 13	VICKSBURG, MI (437.1)	437.1	31.9	6:12	–	4:30	10:18
F 14	VICKSBURG	–	–	–	–	–	–
S 15	VICKSBURG	–	–	–	–	–	–
S 16	[MISS.]	420.0	17.1	3:25	–	7:45	4:20
M 17	[MISS.]	388.5	31.5	7:45	–	5:45	10:00
T 18	NATCHEZ, MI (364.)	364.0	24.5	7:20	–	2:30	7:10
W 19	NATCHEZ, MI	–	–	–	–	–	–
T 20	RILEY'S ISLAND	348.9	15.1	4:00	–	8:40	4:40
F 21	RILEY'S ISLAND	349.0	-.1	-	-	-	2:00
S 22	MILES 313.4 – 313.5 TRAVELLED TOGATHER WITH L'ETOILE DU NORD	313.5	35.5	8:00	–	6:50	10:50
S 23	LAST SAW MITCH + LANCE MILE 304.2	289.0	24.5	6:45	–	6:50	12:05

DATE	STOPS	END MILE	MILES TRAVELLED	BEGINNING TIME	STOP TIME	END TIME	TOTAL TIME
24	FANCY POINT CHUTE	256.4	32.6	6:30	–	8:25	13:55
T 25	BATON ROUGE	229.4	27.0	6:10	–	4:35	10:25
W 26		222.5	6.9	4:30	–	8:10	3:40
27	PLAQUEMINE	209.0	13.5	6:30	–	4:16	10:16
F 28	(194.5)	190.5	18.5	6:30	1:30	8:10	13:40
S 29		176.5	14.0	6:40	–	8:15	13:35
S 30		164.0	12.5	6:40	–	8:30	13:40
M 31		145.5	18.5	6:45	–	8:45	14:00
T 1	HAHNVILLE MET PM + COAST GUARD AUX. UNDER TOW MILE 137.0 AT 12:45	125.0	20.5	6:50	–	4:30	10:20
W 2	UNDER TOW AUDUBON PARK	102.0	23	11:45	–	3:30	4:45
TH 3	MOON WALK (101.3)	94.6	7.4	4:00	:20	6:30	2:10

New Orleans

U.S. ARMY CORPS OF ENGINEERS NAVIGATION CHARTS

The U.S. Army Corps of Engineers publishes detailed navigation charts for major navigable waterways in the United States. These are excerpts from our copy of the Corps' Missouri River charts, with Ed's handwritten notes.

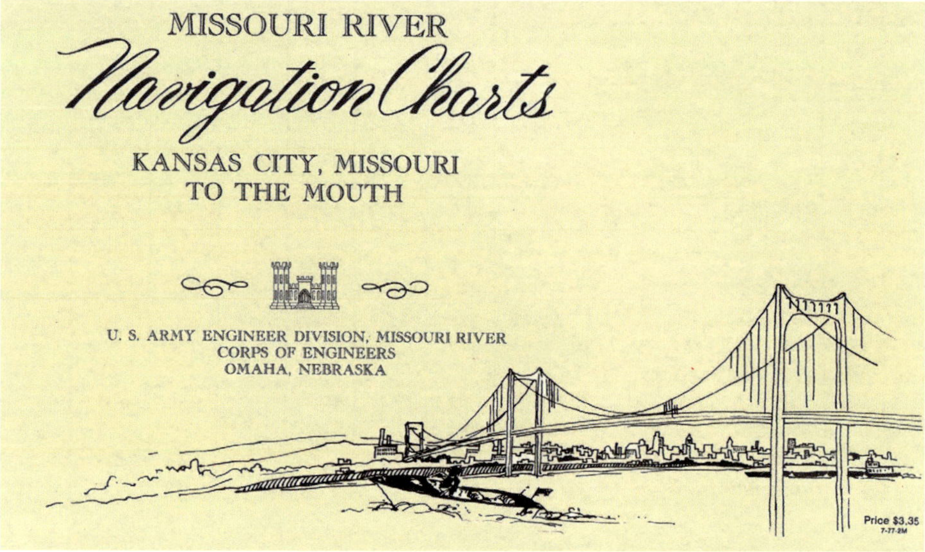

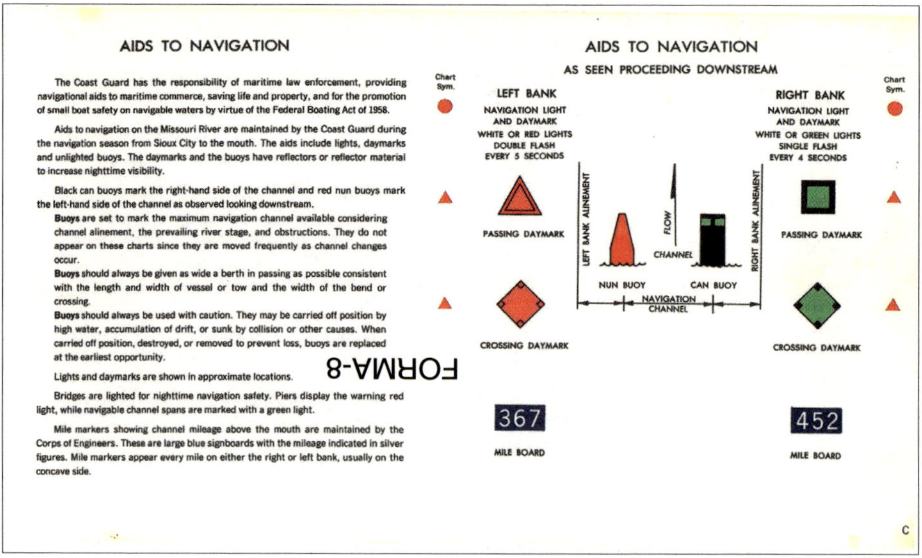

AIDS TO NAVIGATION

The Coast Guard has the responsibility of maritime law enforcement, providing navigational aids to maritime commerce, saving life and property, and for the promotion of small boat safety on navigable waters by virtue of the Federal Boating Act of 1958.

Aids to navigation on the Missouri River are maintained by the Coast Guard during the navigation season from Sioux City to the mouth. The aids include lights, daymarks and unlighted buoys. The daymarks and the buoys have reflectors or reflector material to increase nighttime visibility.

Black can buoys mark the right-hand side of the channel and red nun buoys mark the left-hand side of the channel as observed looking downstream.

Buoys are set to mark the maximum navigation channel available considering channel alinement, the prevailing river stage, and obstructions. They do not appear on these charts since they are moved frequently as channel changes occur.

Buoys should always be given as wide a berth in passing as possible consistent with the length and width of vessel or tow and the width of the bend or crossing.

Buoys should always be used with caution. They may be carried off position by high water, accumulation of drift, or sunk by collision or other causes. When carried off position, destroyed, or removed to prevent loss, buoys are replaced at the earliest opportunity.

Lights and daymarks are shown in approximate locations.

Bridges are lighted for nighttime navigation safety. Piers display the warning red light, while navigable channel spans are marked with a green light.

Mile markers showing channel mileage above the mouth are maintained by the Corps of Engineers. These are large blue signboards with the mileage indicated in silver figures. Mile markers appear every mile on either the right or left bank, usually on the concave side.

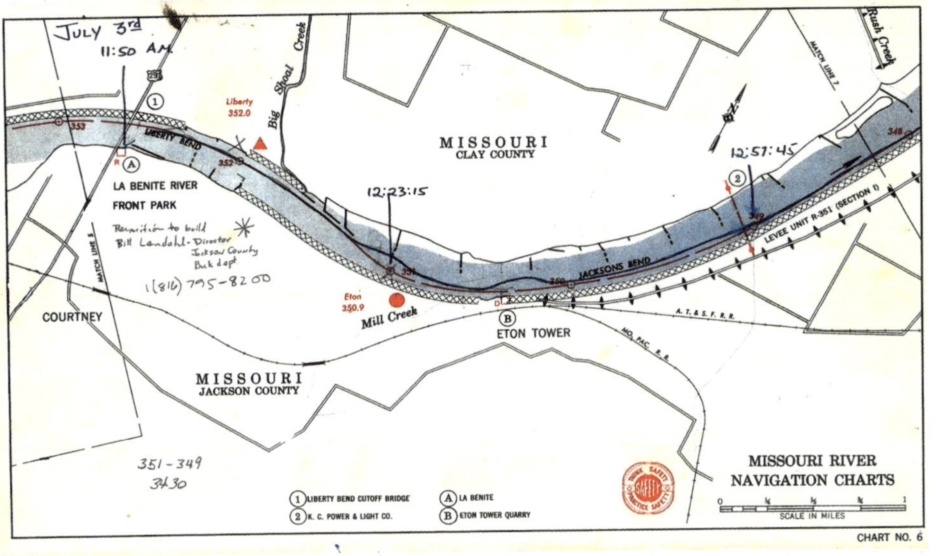
July 3rd
11:50 AM
Rush Creek
Big Shoal Creek
Liberty
352.0
LIBERTY BEND
MISSOURI
CLAY COUNTY
12:57:45
LA BENITE RIVER
FRONT PARK
12:23:15
LEVEE UNIT R-351 (SECTION I)
JACKSONS BEND
Bill Landahl - Director
Jackson County
Park dept
1(816) 795-8200
Eton
350.9
Mill Creek
ETON TOWER
COURTNEY
A. T. & S. F. R.R.
MO. PAC. R.R.
MISSOURI
JACKSON COUNTY
351-349
3430
MISSOURI RIVER
NAVIGATION CHARTS
1 LIBERTY BEND CUTOFF BRIDGE
2 K. C. POWER & LIGHT CO.
A LA BENITE
B ETON TOWER QUARRY
SCALE IN MILES
CHART NO. 6

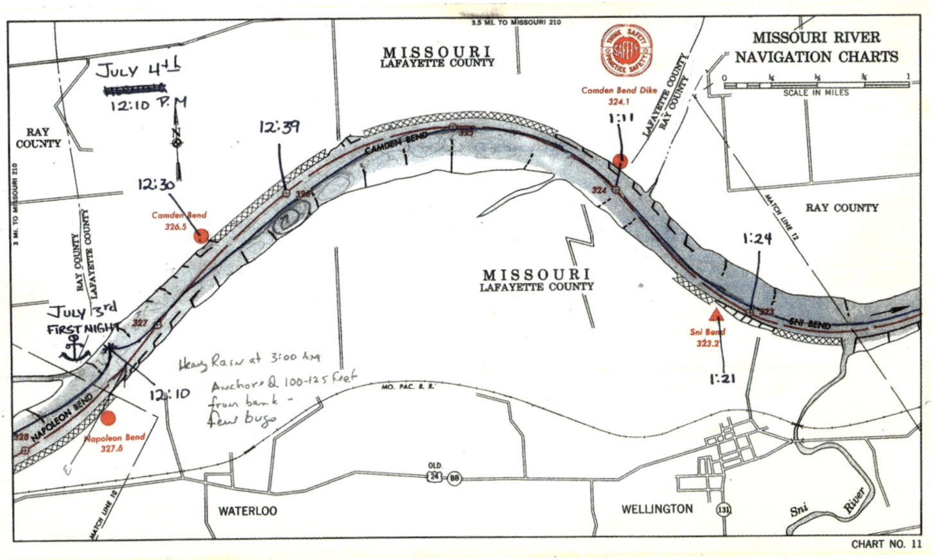
3.5 MI. TO MISSOURI 210
MISSOURI
LAFAYETTE COUNTY
MISSOURI RIVER
NAVIGATION CHARTS
SCALE IN MILES
July 4th
12:10 P.M
RAY COUNTY
12:39
CAMDEN BEND
Camden Bend Dike
324.1
1:11
LAFAYETTE COUNTY
RAY COUNTY
12:30
Camden Bend
326.5
3 MI. TO MISSOURI 210
RAY COUNTY
LAFAYETTE COUNTY
RAY COUNTY
1:24
MISSOURI
LAFAYETTE COUNTY
July 3rd
FIRST NIGHT
Heavy Rain at 3:00 AM
Anchored 100-125 feet
from bank -
few bugs
12:10
Sni Bend
323.2
SNI BEND
1:21
MO. PAC. R.R.
NAPOLEON BEND
Napoleon Bend
327.6
WATERLOO
WELLINGTON
Sni River
CHART NO. 11

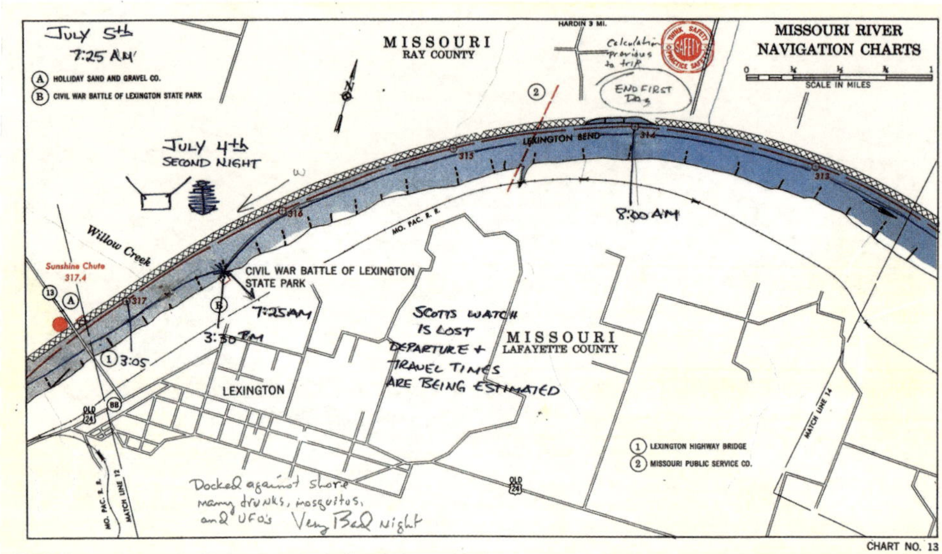
MISSOURI RIVER NAVIGATION CHARTS
MISSOURI
RAY COUNTY
HARDIN 3 MI.
THINK SAFETY SAFETY PRACTICE SAFETY
SCALE IN MILES
JULY 5th
7:25 AM
A HOLLIDAY SAND AND GRAVEL CO.
B CIVIL WAR BATTLE OF LEXINGTON STATE PARK
Calculation previous to trip
END FIRST Day
JULY 4th
SECOND NIGHT
LEXINGTON BEND
315
316
314
313
8:00 AM
Willow Creek
Sunshine Chute
317.4
317
MO. PAC. R. R.
CIVIL WAR BATTLE OF LEXINGTON STATE PARK
7:25 AM
3:30 PM
3:05
SCOTTS WATCH IS LOST
DEPARTURE + TRAVEL TIMES ARE BEING ESTIMATED
MISSOURI
LAFAYETTE COUNTY
LEXINGTON
MATCH LINE 14
MATCH LINE 12
1 LEXINGTON HIGHWAY BRIDGE
2 MISSOURI PUBLIC SERVICE CO.
Docked against shore
many drunks, mosquitos, and UFO's Very Bad night
CHART NO. 13

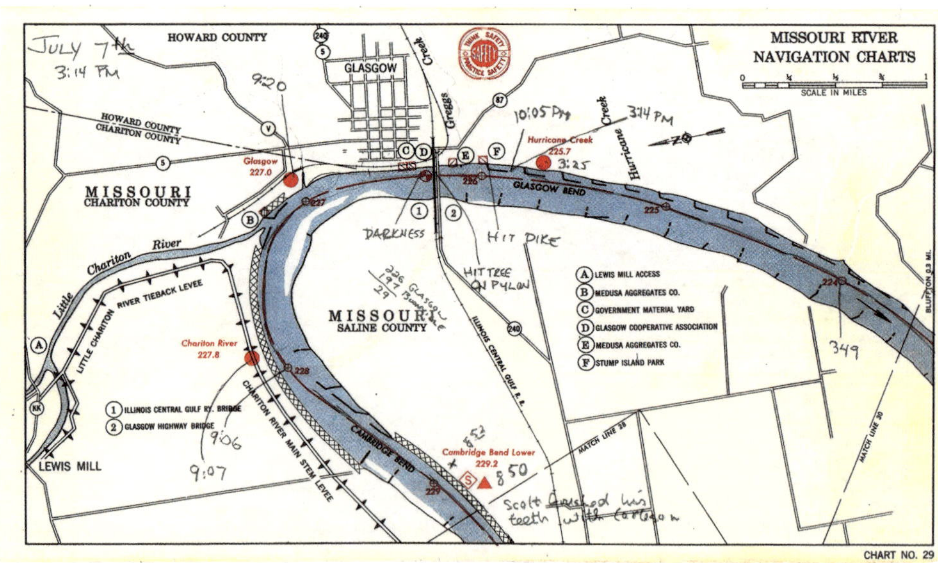
MISSOURI RIVER NAVIGATION CHARTS
JULY 7th
3:14 PM
HOWARD COUNTY
GLASGOW
Greggs Creek
THINK SAFETY SAFETY PRACTICE SAFETY
SCALE IN MILES
9:20
HOWARD COUNTY
CHARITON COUNTY
10:05 PM
3:14 PM
Hurricane Creek
225.7
3:25
Glasgow
227.0
226
GLASGOW BEND
225
MISSOURI
CHARITON COUNTY
Little Chariton River
LITTLE CHARITON RIVER TIEBACK LEVEE
DARKNESS
HIT DIKE
HIT TREE ON PYLON
A LEWIS MILL ACCESS
B MEDUSA AGGREGATES CO.
C GOVERNMENT MATERIAL YARD
D GLASGOW COOPERATIVE ASSOCIATION
E MEDUSA AGGREGATES CO.
F STUMP ISLAND PARK
224
BLUFFTON 0.3 MI.
349
MISSOURI
SALINE COUNTY
ILLINOIS CENTRAL GULF R.R.
Chariton River
227.8
228
1 ILLINOIS CENTRAL GULF RY. BRIDGE
2 GLASGOW HIGHWAY BRIDGE
CHARITON RIVER MAIN STEM LEVEE
9:06
9:07
LEWIS MILL
CAMBRIDGE BEND
Cambridge Bend Lower
229.2
8:50
MATCH LINE 28
MATCH LINE 30
Scott brushed his teeth with Carlson
CHART NO. 29

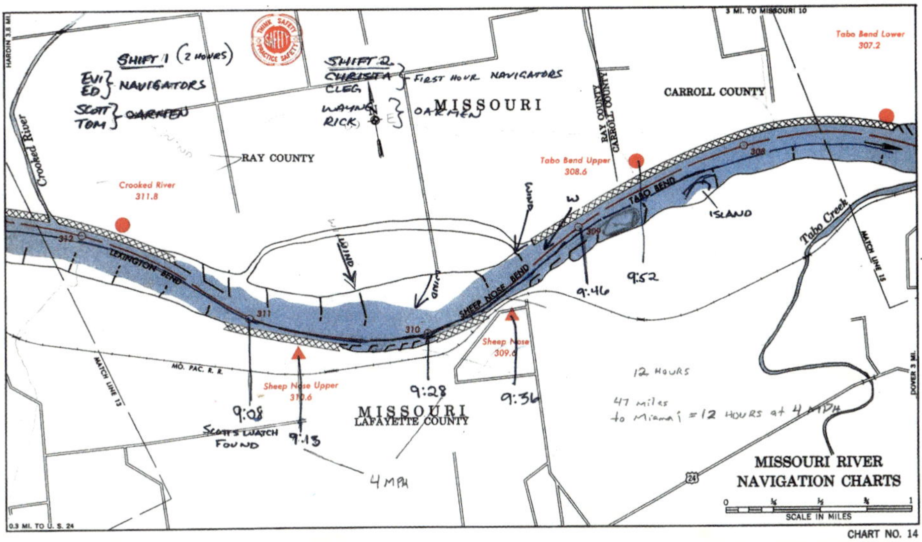
MISSOURI RIVER
NAVIGATION CHARTS
CHART NO. 14
MISSOURI
LAFAYETTE COUNTY
RAY COUNTY
CARROLL COUNTY
Crooked River
Tabo Creek
LEXINGTON BEND
SHEEP NOSE BEND
TABO BEND
Crooked River 311.8
Sheep Nose Upper 310.6
Sheep Nose 309.6
Tabo Bend Upper 308.6
Tabo Bend Lower 307.2
MO. PAC. R. R.
MATCH LINE 13
MATCH LINE 15
SCALE IN MILES

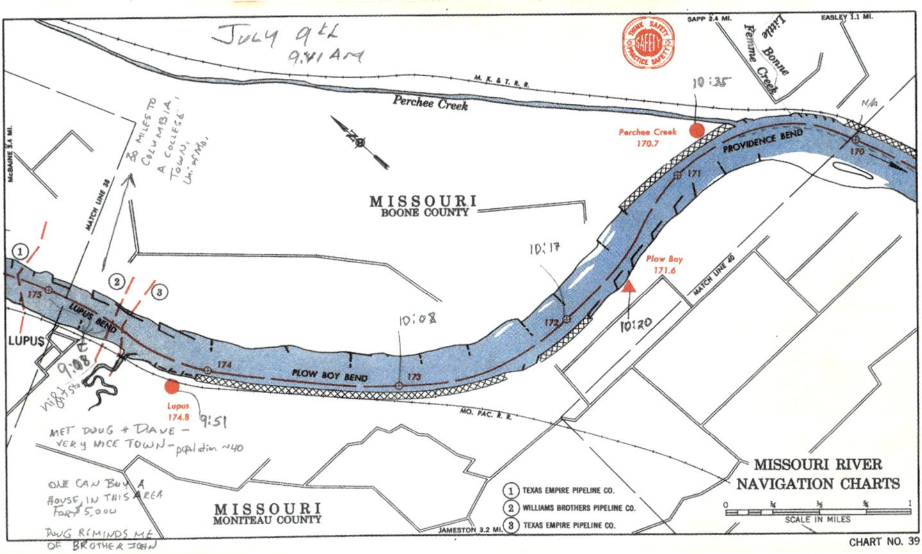
MISSOURI RIVER
NAVIGATION CHARTS
CHART NO. 39
MISSOURI
BOONE COUNTY
MISSOURI
MONITEAU COUNTY
LUPUS
Perchee Creek
Little Femme Bonne Creek
LUPUS BEND
PLOW BOY BEND
PROVIDENCE BEND
Lupus 174.8
Plow Boy 171.6
Perchee Creek 170.7
M. K. & T. R. R.
MO. PAC. R. R.
MATCH LINE 38
MATCH LINE 40
1 TEXAS EMPIRE PIPELINE CO.
2 WILLIAMS BROTHERS PIPELINE CO.
3 TEXAS EMPIRE PIPELINE CO.
SCALE IN MILES

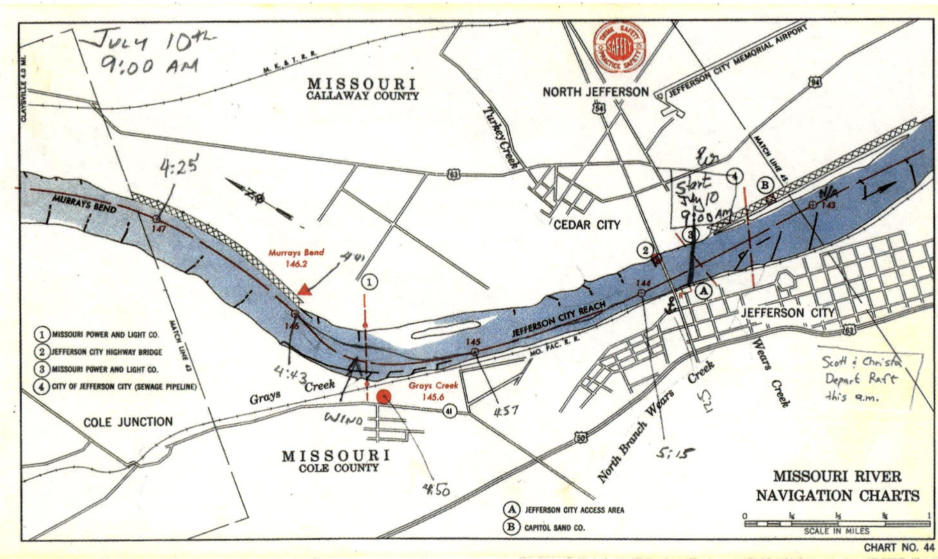
July 10th
9:00 AM
MISSOURI
CALLAWAY COUNTY
NORTH JEFFERSON
JEFFERSON CITY MEMORIAL AIRPORT
Turkey Creek
CEDAR CITY
MURRAYS BEND
Murrays Bend
146.2
JEFFERSON CITY REACH
JEFFERSON CITY
Start
July 10
9:00 AM
Scott & Christa
Depart Raft
this a.m.
1 MISSOURI POWER AND LIGHT CO.
2 JEFFERSON CITY HIGHWAY BRIDGE
3 MISSOURI POWER AND LIGHT CO.
4 CITY OF JEFFERSON CITY (SEWAGE PIPELINE)
Grays Creek
Grays Creek
145.6
WIND
COLE JUNCTION
MISSOURI
COLE COUNTY
North Branch Wears Creek
Wears Creek
MO. PAC. R. R.
4:25
4:41
4:43
4:50
4:57
5:15
A JEFFERSON CITY ACCESS AREA
B CAPITOL SAND CO.
MISSOURI RIVER
NAVIGATION CHARTS
SCALE IN MILES
CHART NO. 44

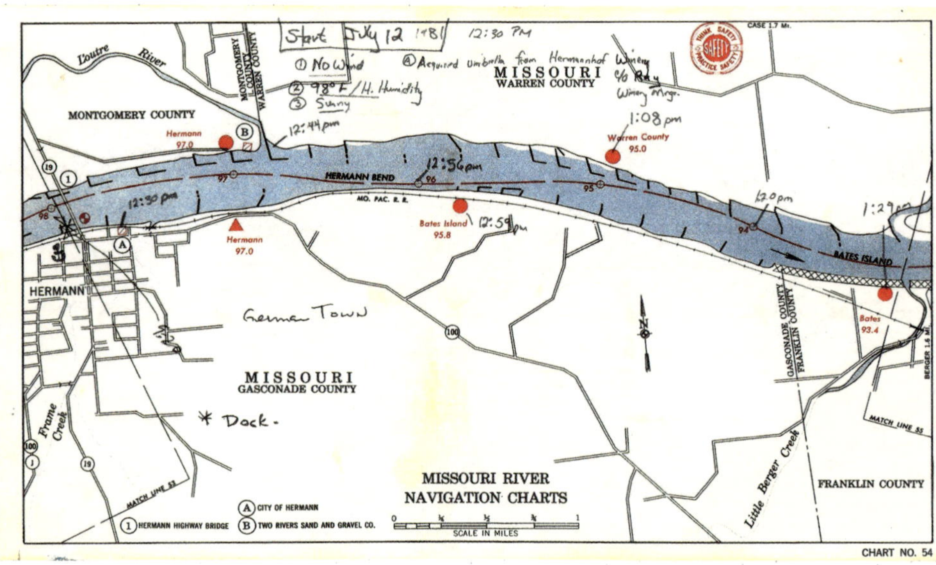
Start July 12 1981 12:30 PM
1 No Wind
2 98°F / H. Humidity
3 Sunny
A Acquired Umbrella from Hermannhof Winery
MISSOURI
WARREN COUNTY
L'outre River
MONTGOMERY COUNTY
Hermann
97.0
12:44 pm
1:08 pm
Warren County
95.0
HERMANN BEND
12:56 pm
12:30 pm
Hermann
97.0
Bates Island
95.8
12:59 pm
1:20 pm
1:29 pm
BATES ISLAND
Bates
93.4
MO. PAC. R. R.
HERMANN
German Town
MISSOURI
GASCONADE COUNTY
* Dock
Frame Creek
GASCONADE COUNTY
FRANKLIN COUNTY
Little Berger Creek
FRANKLIN COUNTY
A CITY OF HERMANN
1 HERMANN HIGHWAY BRIDGE
B TWO RIVERS SAND AND GRAVEL CO.
MISSOURI RIVER
NAVIGATION CHARTS
SCALE IN MILES
CHART NO. 54

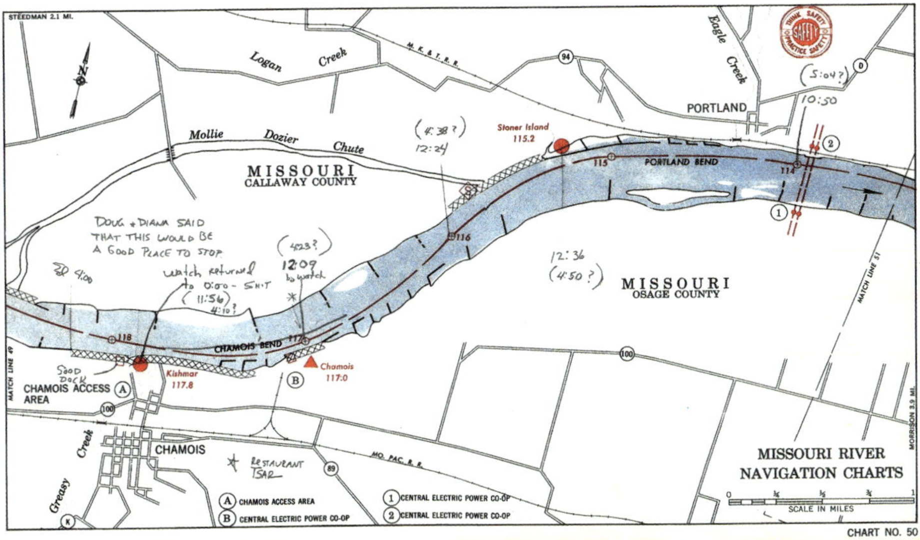

CHART NO. 50

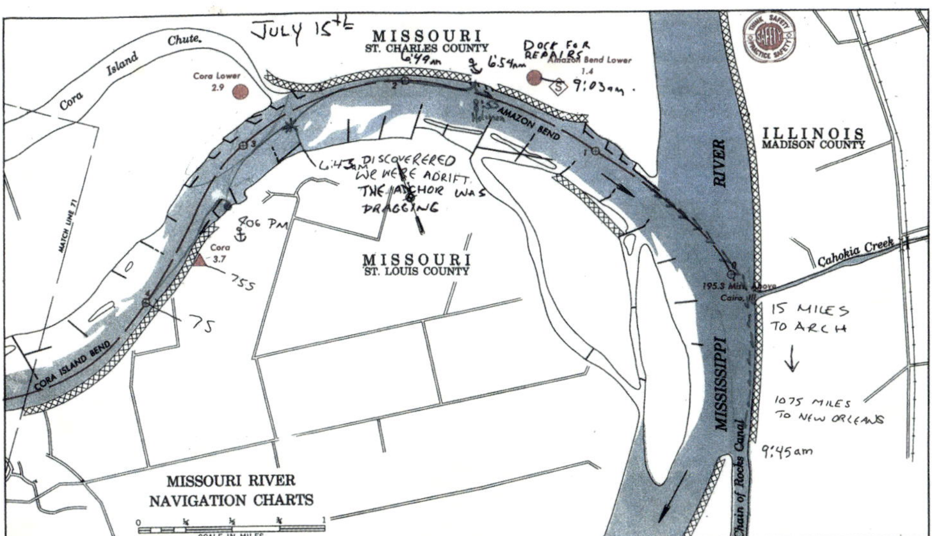

CHART NO. 72